FCE Result

Workbook Resource Pack with key

Paul A Davies & Tim Falla

OXFORD
UNIVERSITY PRESS

Great Clarendon Street, Oxford OX2 6DP

Oxford University Press is a department of the University of Oxford. It furthers the University's objective of excellence in research, scholarship, and education by publishing worldwide in

Oxford New York

Auckland Cape Town Dar es Salaam Hong Kong Karachi Kuala Lumpur Madrid Melbourne Mexico City Nairobi New Delhi Shanghai Taipei Toronto

With offices in

Argentina Austria Brazil Chile Czech Republic France Greece Guatemala Hungary Italy Japan Poland Portugal Singapore South Korea Switzerland Thailand Turkey Ukraine Vietnam

OXFORD and OXFORD ENGLISH are registered trade marks of Oxford University Press in the UK and in certain other countries

First published 2008
2012 2011 2010 2009
10 9 8 7 6 5 4 3

ISBN: 978 0 19 480029 7

Printed in China

ACKNOWLEDGEMENTS

The authors and publisher are grateful to those who have given permission to reproduce the following extracts and adaptations of copyright material: p17 'Happy therapy: Making sense of humour' by John Naish, Timesonline © The Times. Reproduced by permission. pp24–25 'Christo turns the Big Apple orange: Wrappers in New York' by Paul Harris, 13 February 2005 Copyright Guardian News & Media Ltd 2005. Reproduced by permission. pp36–37 'Take a last look at the world, son' by Jane Atkinson from News of the World. Reproduced by permission. pp50–51 'Extreme dining', August 23, 2006 The Guardian Copyright Guardian News & Media Ltd 2006. Reproduced by permission. p60 'The name's Bond – she's the fastest woman to climb seven of world's peaks' by Duncan Campbell, May 25, 2005 The Guardian Copyright Guardian News & Media Ltd 2006. Reproduced by permission. p71 'On the mend', January 15, 2007 The Guardian Copyright Guardian News & Media Ltd 2007. Reproduced by permission. p74 'Where's my jetpack?' by Dean Irvine. Reproduced by permission of Cable News Network.

Although every effort has been made to trace and contact copyright holders before publication, this has not been possible in some cases. We apologize for any apparent infringement of copyright and if notified, the publisher will be pleased to rectify any errors or omissions at the earliest opportunity.

Sources: www.apa.org; http://newsvote.bbc.co.uk

We would like to thank the following for their kind permission to reproduce photographs: Cover photograph courtesy Getty Images/George Doyle/Stockbyte. Apex pp14 (bottom picture/Theo Moye), 15 (man eating carrot/Stuart Quinn); Art Archive pp44 (Gutenberg Press/Gutenberg Museum Mainz /Gianni Dagli Orti), 45 (Samuel Morse/ Culver Pictures); Bridgeman Art Library p47 (Rosetta Stone, c.196 BC, stone, detail, by Egyptian, Ptolemaic Period, [332–30 BC], British Museum, London, UK/ Photo © Boltin Picture Library); Camera Press pp24, 25 (Christo and Jeanne-Claude: The Gates, Project for Central Park, New York City, 1979–2005. Photo: Wolfgang Volz/Laif. (c) Christo 2005); Corbis pp4a, 4b, (Paul-Emile Victor/Richard Melloul/Sygma), 17 (Sion Touhig/Sygma), 30–1 (Bettmann), 38 (bicycle/Gary Edwards/Zefa), 45 (braille alphabet/ Bettmann), 52 (fish/Joson/Zefa), 56 (Rosie Ruiz/Stella Walsh/Bettmann/Tonya Harding/Neal Preston), 75 (C/B Productions), Crown Copyright p14 (top picture/Gary Tyson/MOD), Eyevine p60a, 60b (Barbara Sanders); Getty pp5 (Paul-Emile Victor right/AFP),16 (Ami Vitale), 26 (cookery programme/Manan Vatsyayana/AFP), 38 (hybrid vehicle/Stephen Chernin), 39 (man playing football/Nick Dolding), 52 (chips/Harry Bischof/table/Dorling Kindersley), 67 (Thierry Dosogne), 77 (Abdul Sattar Edhi/Aamir Qureshi/AFP/Oprah Winfrey/ Michelly Rall/WireImage), 81 (Carol Havens); Hendon Times Newspaper p8 (Peter Beal); Oxford University Press pp52 (salt and pepper/knife and fork) ImageState p69; Jupiter Images pp39 (no swimming/Tom Hussey/Workbook Stock), 48 (little boy/Allison V.Smith/Workbook Stock/old lady/Loris Guzzetta/ Nonstock), 51 (Kyle Rothenborg/Foodpix); Magnum Photos pp26 (news bulletin/ Peter Marlow/weather report/Alex Majoli), 71 (Paolo Pellegrin); Mary Evans p49; Millennium Images pp13 (Romain Baillon), 48 (black man/Marysa Dowling), 52 (chair/Tess Hurrell); Minden Pictures p11 (saltwater crocodile/great white shark/Mike Parry/lion/Frans Lanting); National Air and Space Museum, Smithsonian Institution p74 (Bell Rocket belt/SI 2004–18934); NHPA p10 (Andy Rouse); PA pp15 (gorilla/DPA), 35 (Koji Sasahara/AP); PYMCA pp48 (Asian young man/Ben Knight/teenage girl/Josephine Soughan and Simon Pentleton); Rex Features pp5 (Paul-Emile Victor left/Henri Martinie/ Roger-Viollet), 36, 37, 44 (Johannes Gutenberg/engraving P.Stent from R.Gaywood [1650–1711]/Bibliothèque Nationale, France/Roger-Viollet), 45 (Louis Braille/Roger-Viollet), 76 (Bill Gates/Sipa/Albina de Boisrouvray/Villard/ Sipa), 80 (Alex Macnaughton); Ronald Grant Archive pp29 (RKO Radio Pictures), 34; Amanda Searle p21 (Space Cadets); Science and Society Picture Library p45 (Bell telephone/Alexander Graham Bell/morse code generator); Superstock p38 (speedboat/Roine Magnusson); Trek Aerospace p74 (top/courtesy of Trek Aerospace/www.trekaerospace.com).

Commissioned illustrations by: Jon Burgerman pp12, 18; Simon Pemberton p19; Neil Webb/Début Art pp20, 33; Louise Weir p6.

Stock illustration by: Mr Bingo/Zeegen Rush p28; Ryu Itadani/Zeegen Rush pp40–1, 59, 79; Adrian Johnson p21; Peter Mac p72; Joe Magee pp32, 46, 68; Marine/Zeegen Rush pp7, 65; Christian Montenegro/Dutch Uncle p61; Pietari Posti/Début Art p58; Neil Webb/Début Art pp54; Louise Weir pp66, 78.

Contents

1 The circle of life page 4

2 Wild page 10

3 What's so funny? page 16

Review (Units 1–3) page 22

4 Inspired page 24

5 Real or fake? page 30

6 Journeys page 36

Review (Units 4–6) page 42

7 I get the message page 44

8 A matter of taste page 50

9 Going to extremes page 56

Review (Units 7–9) page 62

10 All in the mind page 64

11 Man and machine page 70

12 Make a difference page 76

Review (Units 10–12) page 82

Key page 84

Using the Workbook MultiROM page 103

The circle of life

Reading

Part 1 Multiple choice

1 **Quickly read the text opposite about personality, and decide which of sentences a–c is false.**

a The research was carried out online.
b The research focused on five personality traits.
c The research only involved women.

2 **For questions 1–8, choose the answer (A, B, C or D) which you think fits best, according to the text.**

1 Research on identical twins shows that
  A personality makes people different from one another.
  B people are interested in personality.
  C our personalities change as we grow older.
  D our personalities do not change through life.

2 Srivastava and his team wanted to
  A test a new theory.
  B test an existing theory.
  C carry out a study larger than previous ones.
  D show that they could do research using the Internet.

3 The study
  A looked at people's lives over many years.
  B looked at people's lives over a short period.
  C looked at adults of many different ages.
  D took many years to complete.

4 The results showed that people who are conscientious generally
  A change a lot during their twenties.
  B become less conscientious as they get older.
  C don't change.
  D have unsuccessful relationships.

5 Srivastava thinks that
  A old men are irritable.
  B both men and women get nicer as they get older.
  C women get nicer but men don't.
  D people are generally more agreeable when they are younger.

6 The results of the study
  A correspond with people's actual experience.
  B contradict common sense.
  C tell us that nobody changes.
  D revealed no change in openness.

7 What differences between men and women did the study reveal?
  A It didn't reveal any differences.
  B It revealed that men and women differ in all of the 'Big Five' traits.
  C It revealed differences in early adulthood which lessen as people get older.
  D It revealed that men score higher in two 'Big Five' traits.

8 Srivastava has
  A made further research into personality unnecessary.
  B convinced other psychologists that he is right.
  C made people question the results of previous research.
  D asked for more research to be done.

You're nicer than you used to be

Personality is one of the most interesting ways in which people are different from one another. But where does our personality come from? Are we born with it or does it change as we get older? A great deal of research into personality (notably the studies carried out on twins) indicates that people's personalities are more or less fixed before they are born.

However, not everyone is convinced. Psychologist Sanjay Srivastava and a team of researchers from the University of California, Berkeley, have just completed a large-scale study into personality, via the Internet. Srivastava explains what he and his team were trying find out: 'One of the major theories of personality asserts that personality traits are largely set by genetics, and, by consequence, changes in personality traits should slow as we get older. We set out to test that theory.' The researchers evaluated data from 132,515 adults aged between 21 and 60. The team focused on five personality traits – what scientists call 'The Big Five'. These are:

1 Conscientiousness – how careful, thorough and self-disciplined are you?

2 Agreeableness – how considerate and helpful are you?

3 Neuroticism – how self-conscious and tense are you?

4 Openness – how curious, imaginative and open to new experiences are you?

5 Extraversion – how sociable, assertive and energetic are you?

The huge amount of data, collected over the Internet, allowed for the five traits to be studied across many age groups. What they found contradicted long-held assumptions about when personalities are set. Conscientiousness, a trait marked by organisation and discipline and linked to success at work and in relationships, was found to increase through the age ranges studied, with the most change occurring in a person's twenties. Similarly, agreeableness, a trait associated with being warm, generous and helpful, contradicted the theory that personalities don't change after the age of 30. On the contrary, people in the study showed the most change in agreeableness during their thirties and continued to improve through their sixties. This even happened among men, which debunks the concept of 'irritable old men', Srivastava claims.

The changes in these two traits revealed in the study seem to correspond with the experiences that people tend to have at certain stages of their lives. Common sense tells us that people become more responsible and conscientious as they mature and become better at managing their jobs and relationships. Similarly, agreeableness changes most in people's thirties when many of them are raising a family and take on the role of carers. Openness showed small declines in both men and women over time, a change that indicates less interest in forming new relationships, and reflects the tendency we have as we get older to spend more time with a small group of well-known relatives and friends, and less time going out and meeting new people.

The personality traits were generally consistent between men and women, except for neuroticism and extraversion, with young women scoring higher than young men in both. 'When people talk about The Big Five', Srivastava says, 'neuroticism is probably the one that marks women and men out most clearly from one another – and it's something that's been demonstrated before.' However, the difference in neuroticism is only apparent in youth and young adulthood, and the gap between men and women in both neuroticism and extraversion narrows as people age.

The data collected by Srivastava and his team throws doubt on the conclusion, drawn from studies of twins, that our personalities are largely determined by our genes. The issue is still hotly debated among psychologists, and a great deal more research will be required before the experts are able to agree.

Vocabulary

Relationships

1 Complete the story with the correct form of the verbs in the boxes. Use your dictionary to help you.

Part 1 When Hilary met Sam

ask out chat up fancy get on ~~meet~~

Hilary and Sam first [1] *met* at a party five years ago. It wasn't exactly love at first sight, but Sam [2] .... Hilary as soon as he saw her. However, Hilary spent the whole evening [3] .... another boy. They didn't see each other for a couple of months, then met again by chance at a mutual friend's house. They [4] .... really well and this time Sam seized his chance and [5] .... Hilary ....

Part 2 Is it on? Is it off?

fall in love fall out go out made up split up

They [6] .... together for six months but then they had a big argument and [7] .... with each other. However, after a week apart, Sam realised that he [8] .... with Hilary, and that he didn't want to [9] .... for good. So they [10] .... and started seeing each other again again.

Part 3 A sad ending

break off get back together get divorced get engaged get married propose

Three years ago Sam [11] .... to Hilary. She accepted and they [12] .... Sam bought Hilary an expensive engagement ring. But they kept on having rows and at one point Hilary [13] .... the engagement. Nevertheless, they [14] .... and in the end they [15] .... and bought a flat. But they found living together very difficult and the marriage only lasted two years. They [16] .... last month.

2 Look at the pictures and write the story of Jane and Chris's relationship using verbs from 1.

Grammar

Talking about the future

1 **Complete sentences a–i with an appropriate future form. Use the present simple, the present continuous, *going to* or *will* and a verb from the box.**

arrive	be	borrow	do	finish
have	meet	miss	play	stay

a 'What .... on Saturday evening?' 'I don't know yet.'

b John can't find his gloves, so he .... mine.

c 'What time .... your plane .... in Amsterdam?'

d Pete has decided not to take a holiday this year. He .... at home.

e 'Why are you wearing a tracksuit?' 'I .... football.'

f 'Do you want a drink?' 'Yes, I .... a coffee, please.'

g We should have left home earlier. We definitely haven't got time to get to the station. We .... our train.

h The film .... at ten, so I .... home by 10.30.

i 'What time .... Liam this evening?' 'At eight outside the Town hall.'

2 **Choose the correct future form to complete a–f.**

a By the time I'm 20, I'll *have been studying/be studying* English for 10 years.

b This time next week I'll *be sitting/have sat* on a plane to New York.

c Will you *be seeing/have seen* David this evening?' 'No, I won't have time.'

d When I've finished *The Da Vinci Code* I'll have *read/been reading* all of Dan Brown's novels.

e I'll have *been paying off/paid off* all my debts by 2015.

f Can't you take Saturday off? By then you'll *be working/have been working* for ten days without a break.

3 **Use the verbs in brackets to complete the two conversations below with appropriate future forms. Sometimes more than one answer is possible.**

Gary Have you got any plans for when you leave school?

Eleanor Yes, I 1 .... (take) a gap year. I've applied for a job in Kenya.

Gary Really? Doing what?

Eleanor Well, assuming I get the job, I 2 .... (teach) in a school somewhere.

Gary When 3 .... the job .... (start)?

Eleanor In early September.

Gary So this time next year you 4 .... (live) in Africa.

Eleanor Yes, exciting, isn't it?

Andrea What do you think you 5 .... (do) this time next year?

Robert I don't know. I imagine I 6 .... still .... (work) here. But hopefully I 7 .... (be promoted). What about you?

Andrea I 8 .... (leave) by then. In fact I 9 .... (start) applying for new jobs next week.

Robert Really? I saw a job advertised in the paper that would suit you down to the ground. I 10 .... (bring) the paper in tomorrow.

Andrea Thanks.

Robert I noticed that the closing date for applications 11 .... (be) next week, so you 12 .... (need) to hurry.

Listening

Part 4 Multiple choice

1 **You will hear an excerpt from a radio programme about a woman who has achieved something remarkable at the age of 84. Listen and answer questions a–d.**

a How old was Mrs Schofield when she left school?

b How long has she been studying at college?

c How many lessons does she have a week?

d How many times had she travelled abroad before she started the course?

2 **Listen again and for questions 1–7 choose the best answer, A, B or C.**

1 What did Mrs Schofield learn at school?
- A She learnt to read but not to write.
- B She learnt to make a certain article of clothing.
- C She learnt nothing.

2 What problems did Mrs Schofield have when she was shopping?
- A She could only buy cornflakes.
- B She couldn't read the labels on packages.
- C She only bought things with pictures on them.

3 What impressed her about what the man in the shop said?
- A He achieved success through his own efforts.
- B He had been poor but he became rich.
- C He came to her village and stayed there.

4 What was the experience of going to college like for her?
- A She didn't like the amount of homework she was given.
- B She lacked motivation.
- C It was one of the hardest things she's ever done.

5 Mrs Schofield's plan was to write to
- A her relations in a number of different countries.
- B one relation in the USA.
- C relations with whom she was still in contact.

6 How was she able to find out about local news?
- A She used to ask her neighbours.
- B She had the local paper read to her by somebody else.
- C She used to try to read the local paper.

7 What does she want to do now?
- A She wants to gain the confidence to do anything.
- B She wants to go on a long journey.
- C She wants to carry on learning.

Use of English

Part 4 Key word transformations

1 **Read the dictionary extracts and answer these questions.**

a How does the entry show that a phrasal verb is transitive?

b What symbol is used to show that a phrasal verb is separable (i.e. that the object can be placed between the verb and the particle)?

ˌ**look** ˈ**back** (**on sth**) to think about sth in your past **SYN** REFLECT ON: *to look back on your childhood*
ˌ**look** ˈ**down on sb/sth** to think that you are better than sb/sth: *She looks down on people who haven't been to college.*
ˈ**look for sth** to hope for sth; to expect sth: *We shall be looking for an improvement in your work this term.*
ˌ**look** ˈ**forward to sth** to be thinking with pleasure about sth that is going to happen (because you expect to enjoy it): *I'm looking forward to the weekend.* ◇ [+ -**ing**] *We're really looking forward to seeing you again.*
ˌ**look** ˈ**in** (**on sb**) to make a short visit to a place, especially sb's house when they are ill/sick or need help: *She looks in on her elderly neighbour every evening.* ◇ *Why don't you look in on me next time you're in town?*
ˌ**look** ˈ**into sth** to examine sth: *A working party has been set up to look into the problem.*
ˌ**look** ˈ**on** to watch sth without becoming involved in it yourself: *Passers-by simply looked on as he was attacked.*—related noun ONLOOKER ˈ**look on sb/sth as sb/sth** to consider sb/sth to be sb/sth: *She's looked on as the leading authority on the subject.* ˈ**look on sb/sth with sth** to consider sb/sth in a particular way **SYN** REGARD: *They looked on his behaviour with contempt.*

ˌ**set sth/sb**↔ˈ**back** to delay the progress of sth/sb by a particular time: *The bad weather set back the building programme by several weeks.*—related noun SETBACK ˌ**set sb** ˈ**back sth** [no passive] (*informal*) to cost sb a particular amount of money: *The repairs could set you back over £200.* ⇨ note at COST ˌ**set sth** ˈ**back** (**from sth**) [usually passive] to place sth, especially a building, at a distance from sth: *The house is set well back from the road.*
ˌ**set sb**↔ˈ**down** (*BrE*) (of a bus or train, or its driver) to stop and allow sb to get off: *Passengers may be set down and picked up only at the official stops.* ˌ**set sth**↔ˈ**down** **1** to write sth down on paper in order to record it **2** to give sth as a rule, principle, etc.: *The standards were set down by the governing body.*
ˌ**set** ˈ**forth** (*literary*) to start a journey ˌ**set sth**↔ˈ**forth** (*formal*) to present sth or make it known **SYN** EXPOUND: *The President set forth his views in a television broadcast.*
ˌ**set** ˈ**in** (of rain, bad weather, infection, etc.) to begin and seem likely to continue: *The rain seemed to have set in for the day.* ˌ**set sth** ˈ**in/**ˈ**into sth** [usually passive] to fasten sth into a flat surface so that it does not stick out from it: *a plaque set into the wall*
ˌ**set** ˈ**off** to begin a journey: *We set off for London just after ten.* ˌ**set sth**↔ˈ**off** **1** to make a bomb, etc. explode: *A gang of boys were setting off fireworks in the street.* **2** to make an alarm start ringing: *Opening this door will set off the alarm.* **3** to start a process or series of events: *Panic on the stock market set off a wave of selling.* **4** to make sth more noticeable or attractive by being placed near it: *That blouse sets off the blue of her eyes.* ˌ**set sb** ˈ**off** (**doing sth**) to make sb start doing sth such as laughing, crying or talking
ˈ**set on/upon sb** [usually passive] to attack sb suddenly: *I opened the gate, and was immediately set on by a large dog.*

Oxford Advanced Learner's Dictionary, 7th edition

2 **For each of a–h complete the second sentence so that it has a similar meaning to the first sentence. Use the word given and a phrasal verb with *look* or *set*. The phrasal verbs you need are in the extracts in 1.**

a If you're ever in our part of the country, do visit us.

in

If you're ever in our part of the country, do .... on us.

b I burnt the sausages and caused the smoke alarm to go off.

off

I burnt the sausages and .... the smoke alarm.

c Joe tends to feel superior to people who don't earn as much money as he does.

down

Joe tends to .... people who don't earn as much money as he does.

d A gang of teenagers attacked a man in broad daylight yesterday.

upon

A man .... by a gang of teenagers in broad daylight yesterday.

e The terrible weather delayed the departure of the ferry by six hours.

back

Owing to the terrible weather, the departure of the ferry .... by six hours.

f We all watched in silence as the magician performed his trick.

on

We all .... in silence as the magician performed his trick.

g The house stands about 50 metres away from the road.

back

The house .... about 50 metres from the road

h The police are investigating the possibility that the two crimes are linked.

into

The police .... the possibility that the two crimes are linked.

Wild

2

Reading

Part 3 Multiple matching

1 Read the text opposite quickly. Say in which parts of the world three of the animals are found. Where is the fourth normally found?

2 Read the text again carefully, and for questions 1–15, choose from the animals (A–D). The animals may be chosen more than once.

1 If this animal is about to attack, be as loud as you can. ....
2 If you get close to one of these animals, you should talk to it. ....
3 You should look straight into this animal's eyes. ....
4 This animal is attracted by colourful clothing. ....
5 You should not make eye contact with this animal. ....
6 You're more likely to be attacked by this animal if you show your fear. ....
7 This animal is more likely to attack you if you make sudden movements in the water. ....
8 This animal usually hunts in the dark. ....
9 You can avoid being attacked by this animal if you stand behind a tree. ....
10 If you are attacked by this animal, try to pretend that you are not alive. ....
11 Pretending not to be alive will not prevent an attack from this animal. ....
12 This animal kills its prey by pulling it under the water. ....
13 This animal usually makes an attack then leaves its prey to die. ....
14 This animal can't move as fast as humans. ....
15 Attacks on humans by this animal are becoming more frequent. ....

Predators

A Grizzly Bear

These massive animals can be found in the hills of Canada, Alaska and parts of the USA. Seeing one in the wild is an amazing experience, that is, unless you get too close! If you do find yourself face-to-face with 5 a grizzly bear, what should you do? The main reason that a bear might attack you is if you surprise it. You can help to avoid attack by making some noise when you think you are in a bear's environment. If a bear sees you, begin speaking in a low calm voice and 10 back away slowly. Watch the bear, but don't look it in the eye. Your aim is to show the bear that you are human, and not frightened, but you mustn't appear threatening. Open your coat and try to look as large as possible. If the bear runs at you, do not run away, 15 as it is likely to chase you and you will not be able to outrun it. If the bear does make contact with you, lie down on your front and 'play dead'.

B Saltwater Crocodile

Every year there are hundreds of deadly saltwater crocodile attacks in Southeast Asia. So, how can you 20 avoid an attack from one of these creatures? Firstly,

stay away from water where there are known to be crocodiles, especially at night, when they hunt. And don't dangle your arms or legs off a boat into the water at any time! Avoid surprising the animals – if you see you are going to come near to one, make a noise by slapping the water or blowing a whistle. If you are on land, run from the crocodile as fast as you can, away from the water. Although crocodiles are not as slow as they sometimes appear, they can only run short distances, and even then, a fit human should be able to outrun them. Moreover, their necks aren't very flexible so try to get behind a solid object like a tree. In water, crocodiles tend to drag their prey under and drown them, so if you are attacked, you *must* fight back.

C Great White Shark

Great White Sharks are to be found mainly in Florida, California, South Africa and Australia. They are certainly 'great', growing up to six metres and weighing up to 2,000 kilograms. These animals' reputation as fierce predators is well-earned, but they are actually not responsible for many attacks on humans. However, in areas where sharks are known to exist, there are sensible precautions to take. The best advice is, of course, to stay out of shark-infested waters, especially in the evening and early morning, when most shark attacks occur. If you have to go in the water, carry a weapon, and dress in dark colours. Bright swimwear, and shiny jewellery and watches can attract sharks. Also, avoid splashing in the water. Swim quietly and smoothly at all times. If you splash in the water, a shark could mistake you for a wounded animal and be attracted to an easy target. Sharks bite their prey then move away until the victim dies of its wounds. So, if you are attacked, playing 'dead' won't help you. The best thing is to get out of the water, but failing that, try to hit the shark's eyes and gills.

D Lion

As humans destroy the lion's natural habitats, lion attacks on humans are increasing, though they are still relatively rare. So, here's how to protect yourself when walking in lion territory. Firstly, avoid hiking alone, and never do so at dusk or dawn, when lions are most active. When hiking, make a lot of noise so that you don't surprise a lion. If you see one crouching and hiding, be prepared for a possible attack. Stay calm, look around for something to use as a weapon, and do not run. Make yourself appear larger by opening your coat or holding your hands above your head. Do not crouch down or bend over if you can help it. Stare the lion in the eye and do not look away, while walking backwards and making as much noise as possible. If you are attacked, fight back aggressively, with weapons if possible. If one gets close, punch its nose and eyes. And finally, try to remain standing at all times!

Vocabulary

Finding idioms in a dictionary

1 In most learner's dictionaries idioms are defined in special sections at the end of the entry. Underline the definition of the idiom *get something off your chest* in this entry.

chest /tʃest/ *noun*
1 the top part of the front of the body, between the neck and the stomach: *The bullet hit him in the chest.* ◇ *She gasped for breath, her chest heaving.* ◇ *a chest infection* ◇ *chest pains* ◇ *a hairy chest*—picture ⇨ BODY **2 -chested** (in adjectives) having the type of chest mentioned: *flat-chested* ◇ *broad-chested* **3** a large strong box, usually made of wood, used for storing things in and/or moving them from one place to another: *a medicine chest* ◇ *a treasure chest*—see also HOPE CHEST, TEA CHEST, WAR CHEST IDM **get sth off your 'chest** to talk about sth that has been worrying you for a long time so that you feel less anxious—more at CARD *n.*

Oxford Advanced Learner's Dictionary, 7th edition

2 Read the entry for *tooth* and answer a–c.

a Is the idiom *lie through one's teeth* defined in the entry? *Yes/No*

b Does the entry tell you where you might find the definition of the idiom? *Yes/No*

c If your answer to b was 'yes', underline the relevant part of the entry.

tooth /tu:θ/ *noun* (*pl.* **teeth** /ti:θ/)
1 any of the hard white structures in the mouth used for biting and chewing food: *I've just* **had a tooth out** *at the dentist's.* ◇ *to* **brush/clean your teeth** ◇ **tooth decay** ◇ *She answered* **through clenched teeth** (= opening her mouth only a little because of anger). ◇ *The cat* **sank its teeth into** *his finger.*—picture ⇨ BODY—see also BUCK TEETH, FALSE TEETH, MILK TOOTH, WISDOM TOOTH **2** a narrow pointed part that sticks out of an object: *the teeth on a saw*—picture ⇨ FASTENER—see also FINE-TOOTH COMB IDM **cut your teeth on sth** to do sth that gives you your first experience of a particular type of work **cut a 'tooth** (of a baby) to grow a new tooth **get your 'teeth into sth** (*informal*) to put a lot of effort and enthusiasm into sth that is difficult enough to keep you interested: *Choose an essay topic that you can really get your teeth into.* **have 'teeth** (*BrE, informal*) (of an organization, a law, etc.) to be powerful and effective **in the teeth of sth 1** despite problems, opposition, etc.: *The new policy was adopted in the teeth of fierce criticism.* **2** in the direction that a strong wind is coming from: *They crossed the bay in the teeth of a howling gale.* **set sb's 'teeth on edge** (of a sound or taste) to make sb feel physically uncomfortable: *Just the sound of her voice sets my teeth on edge.*—more at ARMED *v.*, BARE *v.*, BIT, EYE *n.*, EYE TEETH, FIGHT *v.*, GNASH, GRIT *v.*, HELL, KICK *v.*, KICK *n.*, LIE² *v.*, LONG *adj.*, RED *adj.*, SKIN *n.*, SWEET *adj.*

Oxford Advanced Learner's Dictionary, 7th edition

3 For each idiom a–f, decide under which word it will appear in your dictionary. Then use your dictionary to check your answers and find the meaning of the idioms.

a pay through the nose for something
b get on somebody's nerves
c somebody's heart is in the right place
d give somebody the cold shoulder
e put a brave face on it
f behind somebody's back

Grammar

Verb patterns

1 **Complete a–f with the correct form of the verb given.**

a I hope .... law at college when I leave school. (study)

b You spend too much time .... in front of the computer. (sit)

c I dare you .... him how awful his new haircut is. (tell)

d A police car pulled the driver over because he failed .... at the 'Stop' sign. (stop)

e The reason he hit you is that you kept .... him. (annoy)

f Don't put off .... your job application or you may miss the deadline. (send in)

2 **Rewrite sentences a–h using the verb in brackets in the correct form, and keeping the meaning of the sentence the same.**

Example I forgot to lock the door. (remember)
I didn't remember to lock the door.

a Our car is always breaking down. (keep)

b I really don't want to spend the whole summer holiday at home. (face)

c I'm reasonably sure that I'll pass all my exams. (expect)

d Doctors say we should eat less fatty food and more fruit and vegetables. (recommend)

e Try not to hurt his feelings. (avoid)

f I didn't notice that the traffic lights were red. (fail)

g Sue didn't have the courage to tell him the truth. (dare)

h My father hasn't smoked since 1996. (give up)

3 **Complete the dialogue with the verbs in brackets, using the infinitive or *-ing* form.**

Jason Did you remember 1 .... (buy) mum a birthday present when you were in town?

Kate Yes, I tried 2 .... (find) a nice jacket, but had no luck. In the end I got her a new top. Then I stopped at the florist's 3 .... (order) her some flowers.

Jason I bet you forgot 4 .... (get) her a card.

Kate No, I didn't actually.

Jason Can I see it?

Kate Oh, dear. It doesn't seem to be in my bag. I distinctly remember 5 .... (pay) for it. I hope I didn't leave it on the counter.

Jason That's so typical of you, Kate.

Kate Will you stop 6 .... (criticise) me? I'm beginning to regret 7 .... (offer) to go halves with you on mum's present.

Jason Sorry. I didn't mean 8 .... (sound) ungrateful.

Kate You owe me £25 for the top and flowers, by the way.

Grammar Extra

4 **Choose the more likely form of the verbs in italics.**

a I can feel a fly *crawl/crawling* up my arm.

b We sat on the beach for a few minutes and watched the tide slowly *come/coming* in.

c I saw an old man *slip/slipping* and *fall/falling* over, so I helped him to his feet.

d Can you see those men over there *dig/digging* a hole in the road?

e As I walked past the park I saw a group of boys *play/playing* basketball.

f I watched the thief quickly *grab/grabbing* the old lady's bag and *disappear/disappearing* into the park.

Listening

Part 2 Sentence completion

Could you walk 55 miles across this landscape, in just two days, carrying a ten kilogram backpack?

If you think you could, then the Ten Tors Challenge might be for you. Visit our website for more details.

1 **Read the advertisement above and listen to the introduction to a radio programme about the Ten Tors Challenge. Say whether a–c are true or false.**

a The Ten Tors Challenge is a race. ....
b It is open to people of all ages. ....
c The army organises it. ....

2 **Listen again and complete sentences 1–10.**

1 Dartmoor is an area of moorland in the .... of England.
2 Jilly is about to take part in the Challenge for the .... time.
3 The challenge takes place in the month of ....
4 You travel in a .... with five other people.
5 The participants sleep in ....
6 Before the race Jilly was taught how to ....
7 The hardest part for Jilly is crossing the ....
8 On one occasion Jilly nearly lost her ....
9 Last year the event was stopped because of heavy rain and ....
10 Jilly feels that completing the course is a great ....

Use of English

Part 2 Open cloze

1 **Complete sentences a–h with *at* or *to*, or leave a blank if no preposition is required.**

a Maria is .... the hospital visiting her grandfather.
b Shall we drive .... the beach or walk?
c That girl's smiling .... you. I think she fancies you.
d They reached .... their camp at dawn after a 12-hour trek across the moor.
e Don't ever talk .... me like that!
f I asked .... my mum if I could borrow her car, but she said no.
g Don't phone .... me, I'll give .... you a ring.
h The train arrived .... the station early.

2 **Choose the correct preposition in italics to complete the idioms. Check your answers by looking up the underlined nouns in your dictionary.**

a *At/To* first <u>sight</u> I thought that it was a dog running across the field. Then I realised it was a fox.
b Tom can sing *in/after* a <u>fashion</u>, but he hasn't got the world's greatest voice.
c Margaret was so shocked at his rudeness that she was *at/in* a <u>loss</u> what to say.
d I don't want to stop seeing Jenny, but we haven't been getting on well lately, so perhaps it's *to/for* the <u>best</u>.
e *In/On* <u>balance</u> the class's exam results were pretty good.
f I've been *outside/out of* <u>touch</u> with Mark for ages. How is he?

3 **Read the text opposite quickly, ignoring the gaps, and say whether a–c are true or false.**

a The volunteers lived in a zoo for 12 days.
b During the experiment they ate whatever they liked.
c After he left the zoo, Jon didn't change his lifestyle.

4 **Read the text again carefully and think of the word which best fills each gap. Use only one word in each gap. There is an example at the beginning.**

GOING APE

Nine volunteers recently went to live at Paignton Zoo in south-east England, in an area next to the ape house. They were taking part **0** *in* an experiment to be shown **1** .... TV. The idea was that modern diets, which are often full **2** .... processed foods, sugar and fat, cause a lot of health problems. For 12 days, the volunteers, aged **3** .... 36 to 49, ate nothing but raw fruit and vegetables. The diet **4** .... based on research showing that eating as much **5** .... five kilos of fresh fruit and vegetables each day could have a positive effect on cholesterol levels and blood pressure. The reason is that this is the diet our bodies evolved to eat over thousands of years.

Among the volunteers was Jon Thornton, 36, an overweight driving instructor, **6** .... had not eaten vegetables since childhood. Over 12 days, he lost 5.7kg, and reduced his cholesterol **7** .... 20 per cent. His blood pressure also fell. Despite nearly giving **8** .... right at the start when their first meal arrived, he was converted to eating vast portions of fresh fruit and vegetables. 'I didn't feel any loss of energy,' he said. 'I didn't feel ill **9** .... all.'

For Jon, life **10** .... changed since he left the zoo. He has gained a **11** .... weight but now says he only eats when hungry, and he knows that good food can make you healthier and help you live longer. He can now play football because his knees no **12** .... hurt under the extra weight and he goes cycling.

What's so funny? 3

Reading

Part 2 Gapped text

1 **Read the article opposite quickly, ignoring the gaps, and find out**

a where Laughter Yoga started and who started it.
b how long a Laughter Yoga session lasts.
c how many children are entertained by 'clown doctors' each year.

2 **Read the text again carefully, then choose from the sentences A–H the one which fits each gap (1–7). There is one extra sentence which you do not need to use.**

A That's why it doesn't make the drug companies very happy!
B Instead, it's part of a deadly serious form of medical treatment.
C The first two were introduced to a children's hospital in London almost ten years ago.
D Next we do the lion laugh, a yogic practice that involves sticking out your tongue.
E For this reason, most people are reluctant to laugh freely when they are surrounded by strangers.
F But the couple found that their style of humour failed to amuse the Scots.
G In order to achieve this, we play silly games and sing nursery rhymes, breaking down inhibitions.
H It stimulates the body's defences, reduces pain and helps recovery from illness.

Laughter therapy

Whenever you see a group of people rolling about with laughter, you want to know one thing: what's the joke? If Julie Whitehead is responsible for it, the answer is that there simply is no joke. (1) .... Whitehead is at the forefront of moves to make laughter an integral part of the National Health Service in Britain.

Whitehead's movement, Laughter Yoga, was started in Mumbai by a man called Dr Kataria, and has spread to groups around Europe. Several groups and charities, involving comedians, coaches and clowns, are working with health service doctors who realise that joy and happiness have a serious role in the treatment of patients.

Professor Duncan Geddes, a consultant in chest medicine at the Royal Brompton Hospital, says: 'Laughter is an important medicine. It is an expression of happiness, and happiness is good for all of us in three main ways. (2) .... Laughter therapy is developing fast and new research is looking into the ways that laughter happens, how it stimulates the brain and how it makes us all healthier and happier.'

Whitehead says, 'Laughter has wonderful health benefits and, unlike most drugs, there are no side-effects. It's also free. (3) ....' She adds: 'New research at Indiana State University compared groups of people who watched either comedy films or a boring tourist film, and found the group who laughed had their immune system boosted by 40 per cent.'

Whitehead's laughter sessions last around an hour and a quarter. We start by clapping hands, and saying 'ho, ho ho, ha, ha ha', while maintaining eye contact with each other. (4) .... Other exercises involve laughing higher and higher. This can all feel excruciatingly embarrassing, but the idea is that soon it should turn into real laughter.

When Dr Kataria first developed the concept of Laughter Yoga, he tried using jokes. Not everyone, however, laughs at the same gags, so instead the club used simulated laughter exercises. They have the same physical benefits for breathing and circulation. There is also a psychological side, as Whitehead explains: 'We encourage childlike openness. (5) .... It builds confidence and helps you look people in the eye,' she claims.

Meanwhile, 'clown doctors' are being introduced into British hospitals to make sick children laugh themselves back to health. (6) .... I toured the hospital with them in the early days, and was amazed at their warmth and depth of emotional generosity. It takes a lot to bring joy to a building filled with sick children. The project has proved a lasting success and now a team of nine clowns works in a growing number of hospitals, entertaining about 27,000 children and their families every year.

But it's not all 'hee-hee, ha-ha' for pioneers of healthy humour. When Roland Schutzbach and his partner, Christine Fleur de Lys, both from Switzerland, tried to cheer up the Scottish town of Aberdeen, the locals failed to see the gag. Last month, the pair took to the streets dressed in bright red-and-orange wigs, enormous spectacles, huge ties and angel wings at the start of a three-year mission to look for the 'laughter cities' of Europe. (7) .... 'Aberdeen is a difficult case,' Schutzbach admits. 'People did not laugh with us. They did not even look at us.'

Vocabulary

Adjective collocations

1 **Decide which adverb (a–f) goes best with both adjectives in 1–6.**

a perfectly
b desperately
c wildly
d seriously
e stunningly
f bitterly

1 injured/ill
2 disappointed/cold
3 honest/safe
4 beautiful/attractive
5 exaggerated/inaccurate
6 close (e.g. in a competition)/unlucky

2 **Use adverb–adjective combinations from 1 to complete these sentences.**

a 'Do you like my new jacket?' 'To be ...., no.'
b I love the scenery in parts of China – it is ....
c Lewis was .... when he found out that he'd failed the exam.
d The election result was ...., with Henderson winning by only two votes.
e Not only was the newspaper article badly written, but most of the information it contained was ....
f It was a spectacular crash, but amazingly, none of the passengers was ....

Phrasal verbs with *pull*

3 **Rewrite the underlined parts of a–e using a phrasal verb from the box in the correct form. Use a dictionary to help you if necessary.**

pull apart   pull off   pull over   pull through
pull yourself together

a Although he is still seriously ill, doctors expect him to survive.
b When the teacher saw the boys fighting, he separated them.
c As soon as the taxi driver saw the flashing light of the police car, he moved to the side of the road.
d I felt tears coming to my eyes, but I managed to take control of my feelings.
e At 4–0 down, nobody expected the Canadian ice-hockey team to win, but they managed to achieve it.

Grammar

Past tenses

1 **Say which of a or b correctly complete sentences 1–8. Sometimes both are correct.**

1 This is the house where Abraham Lincoln
a used to live. b would live.

2 This town has changed a lot since I've
a been living here. b lived here.

3 You can't say whether or not you like a country unless
a you went there. b you've been there.

4 When Poppy's parents arrived home, all the guests
a left. b had left.

5 Just before 10 o'clock this morning, the bridge
a has collapsed. b collapsed.

6 George still had five shirts left to iron, even though he
a was ironing all morning.
b had been ironing all morning.

7 This is the fifth time
a I tried to call you. b I've tried to call you.

8 This is the old market square where the townspeople
a used to meet. b would meet.

2 **Choose the correct verb form in italics to complete dialogues 1–3.**

1 A: Have you ever been to China?
B: Yes, I have. *I went/I've been* there last year.
A: What *have you thought/did you think* of it?
B: *I've loved/I loved* the countryside but I *haven't liked/didn't like* the cities.

2 A: I'm sorry I'm late. Have you *waited/been waiting* long?
B: No, I haven't. *I've arrived/I arrived* late too!
A: *Has the show started/Did the show start* yet?
B: No, not yet. In fact, only half of the audience *arrived/has arrived* so far.

3 A: *Have you seen/Did you see* Sammy last week?
B: Yes, on Tuesday. *He just arrived/He'd just arrived* back from holiday.
A: Oh, that's right. *He went/He's gone* to Italy to pick grapes.
B: Yes. He told me that *he'd been speaking/he was speaking* Italian so much that he'd forgotten his English.

3 **Complete gaps 1–12 in the story using the past simple or past perfect of the verbs in brackets.**

A man had just got a job as the new boss of a large company. The man that he was replacing met him privately and (1) .... (give) him two numbered envelopes that he (2) .... (prepare) earlier. 'Open these if you run up against a problem you don't think you can solve,' he said.

Everything went smoothly for a while, but after the new boss (3) .... (be) in his job for about six months, sales (4) .... (begin) to fall suddenly and everybody started blaming the new boss. He (5) .... (remember) the envelopes that the previous boss (6) .... (leave) for him. He went to his desk and (7) .... (take) out the first envelope. The message inside it read 'Blame me'.

The new boss called a press conference and announced that all the company's problems were the result of mistakes that the previous boss (8) .... (make). The newspapers (9) .... (print) this, the public responded well and the company's performance improved.

About a year later, the company again started to experience serious problems. Because the first envelope's advice (10) .... (help) him greatly, the boss quickly (11) .... (open) the second envelope. The message that the previous boss (12) .... (write) in the second envelope was 'Prepare two envelopes'.

Listening

Part 1 Multiple choice

1 You will hear people talking in eight different situations. For questions 1–8 choose the best answer (A, B or C).

1 You hear a woman talking to her friend.
Why is the friend angry with Ben, her husband?
A He didn't remember her birthday.
B He spent too much on her birthday present.
C He bought her something she hates.

2 You hear a man talking on the radio.
What is his profession?
A a writer
B a musician
C a film-maker

3 You hear a news reporter describing a major event.
What is the event?
A a celebrity wedding
B a sporting event
C a national election

4 You hear two men talking about a restaurant.
What did they both like about it?
A the large quantity of food
B the fast service
C the cheap prices

5 You hear a singer talking about the start of her career.
How did she use to feel while performing?
A shy
B annoyed
C confused

6 You hear a teenager talking about his family.
What do they all have in common?
A They all love acting.
B They all have a sense of humour.
C They all argue a lot.

7 You hear a police officer talking to a suspect.
What crime has just been committed?
A burglary
B shop-lifting
C vandalism

8 You hear a scientist talking about her job.
What does she enjoy most about it?
A facing mental challenges
B working with interesting people
C knowing that her work is important

2 Listen again and tick the key word that you hear in each situation 1–8.

1	disgusting	....	expensive	....	forgetful	....
2	melodies	....	actors	....	chapters	....
3	politicians	....	guests	....	competitors	....
4	bargain	....	speed	....	portions	....
5	quiet	....	angry	....	puzzled	....
6	rehearse	....	disagree	....	laugh	....
7	graffiti	....	possessions	....	security guard	....
8	significant	....	sociable	....	logical	....

Use of English

Part 1 Multiple-choice cloze

1 **Read the newspaper report below, ignoring the gaps, and find out which of a–c the contestants on *Space Cadets* will really do. Circle YES or NO.**

a go to Russia YES / NO
b travel on the Space Shuttle YES / NO
c appear on television YES / NO

Everybody loves a joke, right? But (0) *what* if the joke is on you? That is what nine unwitting 'thrill-seekers' will eventually discover, having signed up for the experience of a (1) .... – to be blasted off into space in a new (2) .... TV series, *Space Cadets*. It is, in fact, an elaborate and very expensive hoax. The nine contestants – (3) .... three actors planted to help the action along – think that they are undergoing training in Russia, but in reality they're (4) .... the south of England. They believe themselves to be (5) .... against each other for four places on a Space Shuttle flight, but the truth is, they will not leave the ground. Their 'spaceship' will be a prop from a science fiction film, and the flight itself just an illusion created by special (6) .... But is watching a hoax of this kind legitimate entertainment or just exploitation? Practical jokes by their very nature tend to involve a certain (7) .... of cruelty, as they are designed to make the victim feel foolish. But where do you draw the (8) .... between a bit of a laugh and something really nasty? British comedian Arthur Smith says that, in his opinion, drawn-out hoaxes go too (9) .... 'I quite like the idea of briefly fooling a friend, but on an enormous scale like this, it's cruel. The greatest experience of your life is suddenly taken (10) .... from you, and you discover that you've been laughed at for weeks.' Although practical jokes are cruel, they remain popular because we (11) .... pleasure in the misfortune of others, according to psychologists. Basically, we enjoy watching other people look stupid because that (12) .... us feel clever.

2 **Read the text again carefully and for 1–12 decide which answer (A, B, C or D) best fits each gap. There is an example at the beginning (0).**

	A	B	C	D
0	A whether	B how	C (what)	D when
1	A lifetime	B life	C living	D livelihood
2	A truth	B reality	C realism	D truthfulness
3	A together	B altogether	C plus	D moreover
4	A on	B in	C at	D along
5	A wrestling	B winning	C trying	D competing
6	A results	B effects	C causes	D tricks
7	A number	B measurement	C part	D amount
8	A difference	B barrier	C line	D separation
9	A strong	B long	C big	D far
10	A away	B apart	C off	D under
11	A do	B enjoy	C take	D amuse
12	A leads	B causes	C makes	D allows

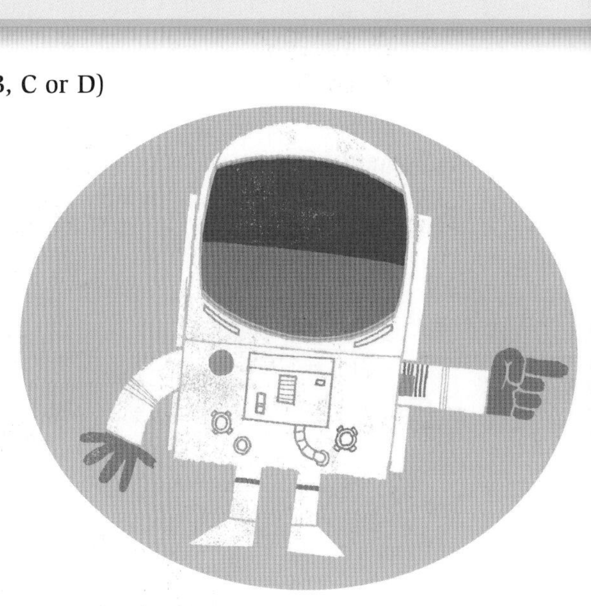

Review Units 1–3

1 **Complete sentences a–h with *back, off, in, on, out, up* or nothing.**

a I wish I was better at chatting .... girls. I can never think of interesting things to say.
b I know that Simon fancies .... Natasha, but he hasn't asked her .... yet.
c Jemima fell .... love with a French boy while she was on holiday.
d Sarah and Harry fell .... with each other last week but I think they've made .... now.
e They got .... engaged in April but the engagement was broken .... in June.
f They get .... very well but they aren't going .... They're just good friends.
g Sam proposed .... to Marianne on New Year's Eve and they got .... married at Easter.
h 'Have David and Lily split .... ?' 'They were apart for a while, but now they've got .... together.'

2 **Put the verbs in brackets into an appropriate future tense.**

Jack How long have you been with the company, Pam?
Pam By next week, I [1] .... (work) here for exactly nine months.
Jack About time you took a holiday then.
Pam Yes, I [2] .... (take) a couple of weeks off over Easter. You [3] .... on holiday soon, aren't you, Jack? (go)
Jack Yes, this evening in fact.
Pam Really? what time [4] .... your plane .... ? (leave)
Jack At nine o'clock. This time tomorrow I [5] .... (sit) by the hotel pool sipping a cocktail.
Pam Lucky you. [6] .... you .... the sales report by the time you leave? (finish)
Jack Sure. I [7] .... it on your desk, if you like. (leave)
Pam Thanks.

3 **Complete the phrasal verbs with *look* or *set* for definitions a–h.**

a feel superior to .... down on
b delay .... back
c visit .... in (on)
d place a building at a distance from .... back
e make an alarm start ringing .... off
f investigate .... into
g watch .... on
h attack .... upon

4 **Rewrite sentences a–e using idioms that include the words given in capitals.**

a Tom paid far too much for his new camera.
NOSE
Tom .... for his new camera.

b Chris says he didn't steal the money, but he isn't telling the truth.
TEETH
Chris says he didn't steal the money, but ....

c I must have offended Rosie because she isn't being very friendly towards me.
SHOULDER
I must have offended Rosie because ....

d I'm sure John has been talking about me when I'm not there.
BACK
I'm sure John has been talking about me ....

e Liam is angry because Kate sold his old camera without his knowledge.
BACK
Liam is angry because Kate sold his old camera ....

5 **Use the verbs in the box to complete the sentences. Use the *-ing* form, the infinitive with *to*, or the infinitive without *to*.**

eat	get	grab	run off	sing	spend	write

a 'Where's Martin?' 'He's in the bath. Can't you hear him .... ?

b I can't face .... a whole weekend with my father-in-law. He really gets on my nerves.

c Lennon and McCartney didn't study music at school, but they went on .... some of the greatest pop songs ever.

d I saw him .... the mobile from the girl's bag and .... down the road.

e 'Did you manage .... the car started?' 'No, I had to call the garage.'

f Do you remember .... at this restaurant last summer?

6 **Rewrite each sentence a–e keeping the meaning the same. Use two to five words including the word given.**

a I can play the piano reasonably well.
fashion
I can play the piano ....

b When I first saw her I thought she was Japanese.
sight
.... I thought she was Japanese.

c We haven't had any contact with our cousins in the United States for years.
touch
We .... with our cousins in the United States for years.

d It's probably a good thing that we couldn't get tickets for the concert. They were very dear.
best
It's probably .... that we couldn't get tickets for the concert. They were very dear.

e Overall I think this government has done a good job.
balance
.... I think this government has done a good job.

7 **Choose the correct adverb in italics to complete sentences a–f.**

a It's going to be *bitterly/stunningly* cold tomorrow. We'd better put the central heating back on.

b Harry was *desperately/wildly* unlucky not to pass his exam. He only failed by one mark.

c It's *seriously/perfectly* safe to swim in the sea here as long as you don't go out to far.

d Most girls think Tom is *perfectly/stunningly* attractive, but I don't think he's that great looking.

e Fears of another wet summer have been *wildly/ bitterly* exaggerated.

f My brother was *seriously/desperately* injured in a car accident last year.

8 **Write the correct phrasal verb with *pull* for definitions a–e.**

a take control of your feelings ....

b get better after an illness ....

c succeed in doing something difficult ....

d separate ....

e move to the side of the road (when driving) ....

9 **Complete sentences a–f with the correct past tense form. Sometimes more than one answer is correct.**

a 'How long .... you .... (learn) English?' 'I .... (start) when I was 12, so six years.'

b Harry wasn't at home when I .... (phone). He .... (just/go out).

c When Pete came in his boots were filthy. He .... obviously .... (dig) the vegetable patch.

d '.................. you .... (ever/go) to Greece?' 'Yes, I .... (go) on holiday there lots of times.'

e My dad .... (write) letters by hand, but now he uses a computer.

f 'Don't forget to phone Jane.' 'I .... (already/phone).

Inspired

4

Reading Part 2 Gapped text

1 Look at the photos then read the text opposite quickly to find
  a the location of the work.
  b the name of the artists.
  c the name of the work.
  d the length of time that the work remained open.

2 Read the text again carefully, then choose from the sentences A–H the one which fits each gap (1–7). There is one extra sentence which you do not need to use.

$21 MILLION

On a cold and breezy Manhattan morning in February 2005, New Yorkers awoke to find their most precious landmark transformed into one of the world's biggest ever works of art. Central Park's dull winter colours of grey and brown became rivers of orange when controversial artists Christo and Jeanne-Claude unveiled their latest project, 'The Gates'. The artwork consisted of 7,500 five-metre high metal gates, each with a huge flag made of orange fabric. 1 ☐ The work was one of the most ambitious ever attempted by the artistic pair, whose previous pieces had included wrapping enormous amounts of fabric around the Reichstag in Germany, a Parisian bridge and part of the Australian coast.

'The Gates' certainly took a long time to complete. Christo and Jeanne-Claude, who live in New York, had first suggested the work in 1979. 2 ☐ At the opening ceremony, thousands of New Yorkers, many of them families, wandered among the gates in a party atmosphere. 3 ☐ 'The Gates' remained open for 16 days and was a huge publicity success for New York. Though the Big Apple rarely needs encouragement to attract media interest, 'The Gates' was exceptional in the amount of attention it grabbed. 4 ☐ The Metropolitan Museum of Art opened its summer roof garden to give visitors a better view. Ironically, the artists themselves had little to say about their project. At the opening ceremony, Jeanne-Claude told the assembled reporters that people should not read too much into the work but should just relax and enjoy it. 5 ☐ Christo explained the pair's refusal to analyse their own work by saying that people should just walk through and enjoy the experience. 'You ask us to talk. This project does not involve talking. It is about seeing. You spend time. You experience the project,'

he said, as he grew visibly annoyed by journalists' questions about the inner meaning of 'The Gates'.

40 In many ways Christo and Jeanne-Claude fulfil a stereotype of modern artists. The mysterious husband and wife team, who are known only by their first names, met when Christo was a penniless Bulgarian portrait artist and Jeanne-Claude was 45 the young daughter of a rich Parisian family. They first began working together in 1960, and their first wrapping project was in 1968 when they used 2,500 square metres of fabric to wrap a building in Switzerland. 6 ☐ Some of their most famous 50 works include surrounding a chain of islands off the coast of Florida with pink floating fabric and erecting 3,100 huge umbrellas in valleys in California and Japan. 'The Gates' certainly followed in that tradition. 7 ☐ As a result, New York's police 55 department used helicopters to monitor the work and added several hundred officers to the park's police force. Typically, Christo and Jeanne-Claude paid the entire extra security bill as well as for the entire work.

A 'It is only a work of art. It has no purpose. It provides no symbol.'

B Aside from attracting a lot of interest and excitement, it also posed a huge security problem and a target for vandals.

C A quarter of a century later, their vision finally became reality.

D But Christo and Jeanne-Claude strongly reject this claim, arguing that artistic value lies in the originality of the concept.

E Other similar projects followed, and the pair gained worldwide fame and a loyal following while maintaining an aura of secrecy.

F These flags created rivers of colour along the park's famous paths.

G One city hotel put binoculars in all its rooms overlooking the park.

H Locals were joined by many tourists, some of whom had come from across America and the world to see the project.

Vocabulary

Television programmes

1 **Match eight of the types of TV show below with extracts a–h from a TV listings magazine. Then label the photos with the remaining three.**

cartoon	quiz show	sports broadcast
cookery programme	reality TV show	chat show
documentary	sitcom	weather forecast
news bulletin	soap opera	

a In the first show of the third series, Jo invites his parents to stay at the flat for a week – with hilarious results. With guest star Steven Martin as Jo's dad.

b Host Kylie discusses love at first sight, with three special guests and a studio audience.

c England v Spain live from Wembley. Commentators Robert Robson and Tony Garbo.

d Six contestants answer general knowledge questions as they compete for big cash prizes.

e Animated fun with Mitch the dog and Kirstie the cat.

f One of the longest-running storylines – Jack and Sanda's stormy relationship – finally comes to an end after six years as Jack leaves Westbridge forever.

g In the last programme of the series, our six students take their final music and drama exams. Will the additional pressure of the TV crew have a positive or negative effect?

h The stunning landscapes of the frozen north of Canada and the wildlife that struggles to survive there.

1 ....

2 ....

3 ....

2 **Find words or phrases in a–h in 1 that are described in a–e.**

a a set of programmes that have the same title and usually the same characters

b a famous performer who makes a special appearance in a programme

c a person who introduces a programme and talks to the guests and/or audience

d a person who describes the action in a sporting event

e a person who takes part in a televised competition or quiz

3 **Complete sentences a–d with your own opinions. Then add one one or two more sentences to answer the questions in brackets.**

a .... is my favourite sitcom. (*Who's your favourite character and why?*)

....

b I think the best reality TV show is .... (*Why?*)

....

c I remember watching an interesting documentary about .... (*What did you learn?*)

....

d .... is the host of a well-known TV programme in my country. (*What is the programme about?*)

....

Grammar

Simple and continuous tenses

1 **Choose the best ending, a or b, for each of 1–7.**

1 Do you know how many times I've
  a been trying to call you today?
  b tried to call you today?
2 Every evening, before going to bed, Jenny
  a is phoning her boyfriend.
  b phones her boyfriend.
3 It was evening, and the birds
  a were singing.
  b sang.
4 Mrs Wilson closed her book, looked up at her husband, and
  a was smiling.
  b smiled.
5 How long have you
  a been waiting for me?
  b waited for me?
6 By the time we find the restaurant, they won't
  a be serving dinner.
  b serve dinner.
7 I can't see you tomorrow because
  a I'm going to the theatre.
  b I go to the theatre.

2 **For each pair a–f, choose the word which cannot normally be used in continuous tenses.**

a	argue	disagree
b	enjoy	like
c	doubt	hesitate
d	cost	pay
e	keep	own
f	realise	learn

3 **Read the email below. Underline 10 mistakes with simple and continuous tenses, then correct them.**

Dear Fiona

How are you? I hope your cold is better and you're feeling OK now. Maybe you're needing a holiday.

I really enjoy my first term at university. I'm now in the fifth week, and I've been making three or four really good friends already. My room-mate, Hans, is one of them. He's coming from Germany. We've got loads in common, and it's feeling as though I've been knowing him forever! The only problem with Hans is that he's liking listening to loud music in the evening when I'm trying to read, but he's always turning it down when I ask him to.

I'll come home just for a couple of days next month to see my aunt, who will be over from the States. I'm not sure exactly when – it's depending on my exams – but I doubt it will be before 15th. It would be great to meet up, if you're free.

Best wishes

Luke

4 **Complete each pair of sentences in a–e with the verb given. Use an appropriate simple tense in one sentence and a continuous tense in the other.**

Example *see*
I'm seeing your cousin tomorrow night.
Now I see why you wanted to come to this club!

a *have*
Don't phone me between 8 and 9 o'clock tomorrow evening. I .... dinner.
When I buy my own house, I .... two cats and a dog.

b *feel*
Your work hasn't been very good recently. .... you .... tired?
After our argument last week, I .... that Leslie and I could no longer be friends.

c *imagine*
I thought I heard somebody outside the door, but when I opened it, there was nobody there. Perhaps I .... things.
I .... that my grandfather will retire soon now that he's turned 60.

d *consider*
Many people .... Pele to be the greatest footballer ever.
Margaret .... giving up university at the end of this term and getting a job.

e *appear*
Two Hollywood stars .... in plays in London next week.
The leading actor .... unhappy in his role and is trying to leave the production.

Listening

Part 1 Multiple choice

1 **Read the first part of each question in 2 below. Decide which two of a–c below you are most likely to hear in each situation.**

	a	b	c
1	a material	b shapes	c melody
2	a special effects	b stage	c stunts
3	a guest star	b rehearsal	c channel
4	a gadget	b electric	c violent
5	a lyrics	b scientists	c research
6	a cameras	b chapters	c audience
7	a moving	b costumes	c stunts
8	a characters	b acting	c plot

2 **You will hear people talking in eight different situations. For questions 1–8 choose the best answer (A, B or C).**

1 You hear two people discussing a piece of conceptual art. What do they both dislike about it?
   A the colours
   B the position
   C the images

2 You hear two guests on a chat show talking about films. What are they trying to agree on?
   A Who is the greatest director ever.
   B Who is the greatest actor ever.
   C What is the greatest film ever.

3 You hear a brother and sister talking about what is on TV. What do they decide to watch?
   A a sitcom
   B a documentary
   C nothing

4 You hear an inventor talking to a bank manager about his latest invention. Why doesn't the bank manager want to invest money in it?
   A He thinks it is too similar to something else.
   B He thinks it will be too expensive.
   C He doesn't think enough people will buy it.

5 You hear a newsreader reporting a medical breakthrough. Who will benefit most from the breakthrough?
   A young people everywhere
   B young people in poor countries
   C everybody in poor countries

6 You hear an episode of a soap opera being made. Why does the director stop the filming?
   A The acting is not very natural.
   B It's too dark in the studio.
   C The actors are moving around too much.

7 You hear a woman talking to her friend about a dance performance. What was the best thing about it, in her opinion?
   A the ending
   B the special effects
   C the music

8 You hear a novelist talking to an interviewer about the process of writing. What does the novelist do when she can't think of any ideas?
   A She stays at her desk.
   B She goes somewhere quiet.
   C She has a coffee somewhere busy.

Use of English

Part 2 Open cloze

1 Complete sentences a–h with the correct articles (*a*, *an* or *the*), or leave the gap blank if no article is required.

a Orson Welles was born in .... USA.

b His father was .... inventor and his mother was .... pianist.

c As .... child, Welles learned to play .... piano.

d After .... death of his mother, Welles abandoned his interest in .... music.

e In his youth, Welles travelled around .... world.

f He had .... great voice for radio.

g At the request of .... US government, Welles made .... documentary about .... South America.

h .... documentary was intended to improve international relations.

2 Read the text below, about Orson Welles, to find three things (a–c) he created.

a series of books b radio programme c film

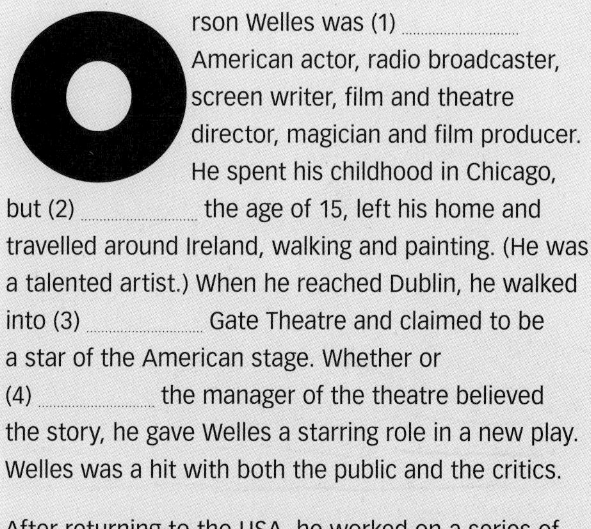

Orson Welles was (1) .... American actor, radio broadcaster, screen writer, film and theatre director, magician and film producer. He spent his childhood in Chicago, but (2) .... the age of 15, left his home and travelled around Ireland, walking and painting. (He was a talented artist.) When he reached Dublin, he walked into (3) .... Gate Theatre and claimed to be a star of the American stage. Whether or (4) .... the manager of the theatre believed the story, he gave Welles a starring role in a new play. Welles was a hit with both the public and the critics.

After returning to the USA, he worked on a series of books called *The Mercury Shakespeare*, which were bestsellers (5) .... decades. But he achieved worldwide fame in 1938 with his radio adaptation of the famous science fiction story, *The War Of the Worlds*. The programme was in the style of a news bulletin, and thousands of listeners panicked, believing (6) .... aliens from Mars really (7) .... invaded the Earth.

At the age of 26, Welles wrote, directed, produced and starred in a film (8) .... *Citizen Kane*, which many film critics consider to (9) .... the greatest film ever made. His acting was powerful and convincing. In one scene, his character becomes (10) .... furious that he destroys a room (11) .... his bare hands. After this scene, Welles apparently walked off the set with blood on his hands, saying (12) .... himself 'I felt it. I felt it.'

ORSON WELLES

3 Read the text again carefully, and think of the word which best fits each gap. Use only one word in each gap.

Real or fake?

5

Reading

Part 3 Multiple matching

1 Read the text opposite quickly and tick the sentence which most accurately describes the writer's opinion about UFOs.

a He definitely doesn't believe in them. ....

b He definitely believes in them. ....

c He has an open mind about them. ....

2 Read the text again carefully, and for questions 1–15, choose from the reports of UFO sightings (A–D). The reports may be chosen more than once.

In which reported sighting

1 did a witness claim that aliens made contact with him?
2 did witnesses claim to see three alien spacecraft?
3 did the UFO apparently injure the witness?
4 was the witness working at night when he saw the UFO?
5 did a witness see a UFO from the building in which he was working?
6 did the witness report seeing an alien on a spacecraft?
7 did an animal get killed or injured?
8 did a member of the witness' family report the incident?
9 did the witness realise that what they had seen wasn't a UFO?
10 did a witness claim that a UFO had moved at high speed?
11 did people advise the witness not to say anything about what he'd seen?
12 did a witness contact Nick Pope the moment he saw the UFO?
13 did the witness hear the UFO before it became visible?
14 did the UFO appear above a sports field?
15 did reports of a sighting come from a number of places?

Is there anybody out there?

Between 1991 and 1994 Nick Pope worked at the British Ministry of Defence investigating UFOs. He received 2–300 reports each year, of which around 90% could 5 **be explained. For the other 10% he could find no rational explanation ...**

Sighting A

The first call came from a police officer. He and his colleague had been on a routine patrol the night before and had seen a UFO. The officer was often on 10 duty at night and was used to the sights and sounds of the darkness. But what he and his colleague had seen was like nothing they had come across before. This was no shooting star, no meteor. Two bright lights, with a third, fainter one, were flying 15 in perfect formation across the sky. I questioned the officer carefully over the phone. From what he told me about their colour and movement, they were not aircraft lights or fireballs. They were simply unidentifiable. As the morning wore on, the calls 20 came thick and fast from other parts of the country.

Most sightings had occurred between 1 and 1.30 am with particular concentration at 1.10 am. One of the sightings was from a man with vast experience of aeroplanes and mathematics. He had watched 25 the objects flying low over the coast and had timed their passage between two points on the shoreline; he was able to calculate their speed at about 1,100 mph.

Sighting B

There is usually a delay between a sighting and 30 when a witness decides to contact someone 'official'. In the case of the 'Capital' sighting, things were rather more immediate. The call came from Capital Radio's headquarters in London and the voice was very excited. The caller was staring out 35 of his window, giving me a commentary on a UFO about to land in Regent's Park. There was hysteria in his voice. 'It's almost down ... it looks a bit like – like a big kite, but it can't be. It's down! It's down! My God, people are gathering around it ... .' There 40 was a pause. The voice seemed less strained, less panicked. 'It can't be a kite, can it? Oh, the people are putting it back in a box. It is a kite. Sorry for having wasted your time.' He hung up. Goodness knows what agonies he had gone through in 45 those few mad minutes. Goodness knows how embarrassed he is at the memory of it.

Sighting C

In the early hours of 29th October 1993, something took place which I was utterly at a loss to explain. The witness was a young naval officer trained in 50 careful observation. He saw a bright object glowing eerily in the sky as it hovered silently over a football pitch behind his home. Its shape was clearly that of a disc and it appeared solid, with rows of different-coloured lights. The witness claimed that 55 he received telepathic messages, telling him not to be afraid. The craft's lights had by this time gone out and it hovered in front of a set of goalposts. A large bird, presumably a rook or crow, flew close to the object, then fell to the ground. The officer ran 60 to wake his family, who saw the bird on the ground but no sign of the craft. Even the bird had gone by the next morning. The officer was confused by what he had seen and reported the incident to the police the next day. They in turn contacted me. The 65 officer's superiors at the college allegedly told him to keep quiet. I suspect the advice was well meant, to shield him from ridicule. I was unable to come up with any explanation.

Sighting D

In 1992 I received a letter from a woman whose 70 husband had been walking in the hills four years earlier, photographing the scenery. The sky was clear, the air still. The woman said that her husband reported a deep rumbling sound ahead of him and above, and saw a huge black craft moving towards 75 him, its body saucer-shaped but with two bat-like wings. It hovered for about five minutes, close enough for the witness to see that the main part of the craft had two decks. He could even make out a small figure, wearing some kind of helmet, 80 through the windows on one of the decks. The craft flew slowly directly overhead, no more than 50 feet above the ground. Instinctively he threw himself to the ground and as the shadow passed over him, he felt a burning sensation. When he got home, he 85 discovered that his clothes had been singed. No explanation was ever found.

Vocabulary

Expressing probability

1 Complete the expressions in the chart with words from the box.

against	bound	chance	chances
doubt	doubt	inevitable	likely
no way	odds	unlikely	

Certain to happen	*It's .... that …* *It's .... to …* *There's no .... that …*
Almost certain to happen	*It's .... that …* *The .... are that …* *The .... are that …*
Not at all certain to happen	*It's .... that …* *I .... that …* *The odds are .... …*
Certain not to happen	*There's no .... that …* *There's .... (that) …*

2 Rewrite sentences a–h using the word given in bold and keeping the same meaning.

a Sandra and Tom will probably get married in the summer.
odds

....

b I'm sure Philip will be late.
bound

....

c It's likely that you'll be stopped by the police if you drive that fast.
chances

....

d It's unlikely that this government will win the next general election.
odds

....

e I'm definitely not taking the blame for the accident.
way

....

f I don't think Andrew will pass all his exams.
doubt

....

g The climate is bound to change a lot over the next 100 years.
inevitable

....

h We're certain to rely increasingly on computers in the coming years.
doubt

....

Grammar

Reported speech

1 **For sentences a–f report the information, using the verb given in capitals and an infinitive.**

a 'I won't lose my temper so often,' said Mike.
PROMISE

....

b 'I can give Theo a lift to the station,' said Martin.
OFFER

....

c 'Where shall I park?' said Joanna to Sam.
ASK

....

d 'Please don't leave me!' said William to Jessica.
BEG

....

e 'Don't go out alone after dark,' said Richard to Kirsty.
WARN

....

f 'I wouldn't buy those shoes.' said Karen to David.
ADVISE

....

2 **Correct the mistakes in sentences a–e.**

a My sister said me that she was going to town.
b I asked her if she will buy me a newspaper.
c She asked me which newspaper did I want.
d I told her I want a copy of the *Independent*.
e On her return she told me she can't find one.

3 **Complete the reported speech in sentences a–g.**

a 'I don't want to go to the leisure centre with you tomorrow,' said Sarah to Chris.
Sarah told ....

b 'We haven't lost a single match all season,' said Fred.
Fred boasted ....

c 'Why didn't you phone me last night?' he asked her.
He asked ....

d 'You're always interrupting me!' she told him.
She complained ....

e 'Have you ever been to Rome?' she asked him.
She asked ....

f 'Your postcard arrived yesterday,' she told him.
She said ....

g 'How often does Tom go to the gym?' she asked me.
She ....

Listening

Part 4 Multiple choice

1 **You are going to listen to someone being interviewed about a famous radio programme broadcast in the USA. Listen once and say which of a–c is true.**

a The radio programme aimed to frighten people but failed because it was a documentary, not a drama.

b People realised that they were listening to a drama but were frightened because it was so realistic.

c The radio programme caused panic among many listeners, who believed that the dramatised events were actually taking place.

2 **Listen again and for questions 1–7, choose the best answer (A, B or C).**

1 The broadcast by Orson Welles was
 A based on a book by Rachel Watson.
 B based on a book by an English novelist.
 C an original piece of work.

2 In the story
 A aliens come to Earth from Mars.
 B enormous fighting machines travel from Mars.
 C the people of London build machines to defend themselves.

3 What was Orson Welles known for at the time of the broadcast?
 A writing film screenplays
 B directing films
 C directing plays and radio programmes

4 Why does Rachel think that many listeners believed the news reports?
 A The action was set in places they knew.
 B The programme makers didn't warn listeners that the reports weren't real.
 C Listeners didn't notice the warnings.

5 Why were people worried about gas?
 A They believed the Martians were using it to attack people.
 B Some people fled their homes and left the gas on.
 C It was impossible to smell it.

6 Why does Rachel believe the listeners weren't stupid?
 A The news reports were very realistic and believable.
 B They weren't used to hearing news like that on the radio.
 C Radio was new and people weren't used to it.

7 What did the radio station promise to do?
 A Warn listeners properly next time.
 B Never use fake news reports again.
 C Stop making drama programmes.

Use of English

Part 3 Word formation

1 Look at the pairs of words in a–f and match the prefixes with meanings 1–6 below.

a **mis**
misunderstand misbehave

b **re**
rebuild rearrange

c **under**
undercooked underestimate

d **semi**
semicircle semi-final

e **anti**
anticlockwise antisocial

f **over**
overoptimistic overeat

1 against or the opposite of
Prefix ....

2 wrongly or badly
Prefix ....

3 more than usual or too much
Prefix ....

4 again
Prefix ....

5 less than usual or not enough
Prefix ....

6 half
Prefix ....

2 Read the text on the right and complete gaps 1–10 with words formed from those given. Gaps 3 and 5 use prefixes from 1 above.

0 *fascinate*
1 recent
2 exist
3 think
4 discover
5 climax
6 success
7 nature
8 rare
9 deep
10 behave

monsters from the deep

Tales of giant sea monsters have been common for many centuries, inspiring fear and (0) *fascination* among sailors. However, until comparatively (1) .... there was no firm evidence for the (2) .... of such creatures. Towards the end of the nineteenth century, a number of dead giant squid were washed up on the shores of Newfoundland, which forced scientists to entirely (3) .... their opinion. The (4) .... of the dead animals spurred marine scientists to redouble their efforts to capture a live specimen. However, all their attempts ended in failure and (5) .... Then, in 2004 two Japanese researchers were (6) .... in taking the first ever photos of a giant squid in its (7) .... habitat. They were astonished by what they saw. Up until that point, scientists had thought that squids (8) .... moved and simply ate whatever drifted by, but the photos revealed that they had misunderstood the nature of these enormous creatures. Taken at a (9) .... of 900 metres off Japan's Ogasawara Islands, the pictures show the squid aggressively attacking bait on a line that the researchers had dropped from their boat. Marine scientists worldwide are now eager to discover more about the nature and (10) .... of giant squid.

Journeys

6

Reading

Part 1 Multiple choice

1 **Read the text below quickly and do the following.**

a Number these countries in the order in which Asa visited them.

Canada ☐ Egypt ☐ France ☐ New Zealand ☐ Thailand ☐

b Find three methods of transport mentioned in the text.

Last chance to see the world

Thirteen-year-old Asa Singleton sits in his bedroom and smiles as he looks through his holiday photos – photos that tell the moving story of a mother and father's love for their boy, and of a breathtaking race against time. For Asa will be blind by the end of the year – and so his parents, Paul and Debbie, sold their business to give him the greatest gift they could: to let their son see the world. 'We wanted him to have the experience of a lifetime before he loses his sight,' says Paul. 'And we did it all just in time.'

Asa was just a few months old when doctors diagnosed that he had been born with the incurable condition NF2, which begins to cause damage to the nervous system from an early age, often leading to deafness and blindness. 'We'd always planned a dad-and-son world trip when he was 16 – but I knew it would be too late by then,' says Paul, 46. 'So Debbie and I made the decision that we should go as soon as it was possible.'

'It was all a bit nerve-racking because of the unpredictability of Asa's condition,' says Paul. 'At home, his sight wasn't such a problem because he knew where everything was. Away from home, we knew it would be more difficult. And he was a little frightened about going to so many strange places. But as soon as we arrived at our first destination, Paris, and saw the Eiffel Tower, we forgot our fears. It was so exciting, being at the beginning of an amazing, life-changing journey.' From France, they travelled to Germany, Italy, Cyprus and then Egypt.

'A guide took us to the top of a Pyramid, and the view was breathtaking. We could see the desert going on forever. It was a sight neither of us will ever forget,' says Paul. 'In Japan we went to Mount Fuji and stayed in a traditional Japanese hotel. It was fascinating, although Asa wasn't too impressed with the sushi that we had for dinner. We travelled on the underground system in Tokyo, which was quite scary for Asa with his poor sight, but he was determined to try it.'

In Hawaii, dad and son went whale watching; and in Thailand, Asa bottle-fed a tiger cub. But his favourite part of the journey was seeing the island where the *James Bond* film *The Man with the Golden Gun* was filmed. 'Asa's a huge *Bond* fan, so there was no way we could go to Thailand without seeing James Bond Island.'

What astonished Paul most on the trip was his son's fearlessness, despite being hardly able to see. 'All his life, he's deliberately taken on tough physical challenges,' says Paul. 'But I was terrified when he said he wanted to go skydiving over the Great Barrier Reef when we got to Australia. I jumped first, and kept looking behind me until I saw his parachute open. I needn't have worried, though. He was absolutely fine, and he loved every second of it. He was so proud of himself.'

Asa also enjoyed the quiet moments of the trip. 'Our longest stop was New

2 Read the text again carefully and for questions 1–8, choose the answer (A, B, C or D) which you think fits best according to the text.

1 Why did Asa's parents arrange a round-the-world trip for him?
   A They wanted him to see the world before he lost his eyesight.
   B They had sold their business and wanted to spend the money on their son.
   C They wanted to share the experience of a lifetime with him.
   D They thought the journey might improve his medical condition.

Zealand, where we celebrated Christmas. We hired a camper van and spent a month sleeping under the stars
85 in Auckland,' says Paul. 'There was something about the solitude and beauty of the place that he really connected with. He also went swimming with dolphins there.'

Next stop was the USA. Paul and Asa stayed a few days at a ranch near the Grand Canyon and went on to visit Las
90 Vegas, Dallas, New Orleans, and take a boat trip down the Mississippi River. Then it was over to Florida to meet up with mum Debbie and Asa's sister Dominique, 17, for a holiday together. Finally they all headed off to Toronto in Canada to catch the flight home.

95 When Asa had his next hospital checks, the news wasn't good. His eyesight has deteriorated rapidly, and Asa is now registered blind. Paul says: 'If we'd waited any longer, it would have been too late and he would have missed out on the experience of a lifetime.'

2 People suffering from NF2
   A are born with damaged nervous systems.
   B are usually deaf from birth.
   C develop the condition when they are only a few months old.
   D often lose their sight and hearing.

3 Why were Asa's parents more worried about his sight problems during the trip than before it?
   A Asa himself felt frightened during the trip.
   B They knew his eyesight was getting worse all the time.
   C His sight problems mattered less in familiar surroundings.
   D Asa's reactions were difficult to predict.

4 Seeing the Eiffel Tower was particularly exciting because
   A it made them forget their worries.
   B they knew it was the start of an incredible trip.
   C they knew it would change their lives.
   D they knew they would be going to Germany next.

5 One thing that Asa did was not very keen on was
   A the huge size of the desert.
   B the traditional hotel near Mount Fuji.
   C some of the food in Japan.
   D the journey to Tokyo.

6 How did Asa and his father react to parachuting in Australia?
   A Asa loved it, but Paul was worried about his son.
   B Paul enjoyed it, but Asa found the physical challenge too tough.
   C They were both completely fearless.
   D They were both terrified at first, but enjoyed it in the end.

7 Asa really enjoyed his time in New Zealand because
   A it was a great place to spend Christmas.
   B he could look at the stars at night.
   C he saw some interesting wildlife there.
   D he loved being in such attractive and peaceful surroundings.

8 What did Asa do in Florida?
   A He caught the flight home to England.
   B He went on a boat.
   C He spent some time with the rest of his family.
   D He spent a few days on a ranch.

Vocabulary

Vehicles

1 Tick the parts which each vehicle below usually has. Use a dictionary to help you.

	bicycle	car	speedboat
boot			
brakes			
engine			
handlebars			
ignition			
roof			
saddle			
steering wheel			
tyres			
windscreen			

2 Complete sentences a–f with words from 1.

a My dad keeps a first-aid kit in the .... of his car.

b Mountain bikes are better for rough terrain than road bikes because they have wider, thicker ....

c I'm not surprised your speedboat was stolen – you always leave the key in the .... !

d As he approached the junction, he tried to slow down but, to his horror, found that his .... weren't working.

e His passenger reached across and grabbed the .... just before they hit the wall.

f My bike hit the kerb and stopped, and I flew over the .... onto the pavement.

3 Complete sentences a–f with the correct verb in an appropriate form.

a We missed the turning the first time, so turned the car around and ....
go back reverse

b I was too late. Just as I reached the platform, the train ....
pull away pull up

c Most people slow down when they .... a police car waiting by the side of the road.
overtake pass

d The bus driver lost control of his vehicle and .... a lamppost.
crash hit

e As she drove past the accident, a piece of glass on the road .... one of her tyres.
break puncture

f A sudden gust of wind made her .... into the middle of the road.
steer swerve

Grammar

Modal verbs: advice, ability, prohibition and obligation

1 Match sentences a–f with the sentences which follow them (1–6), and choose the correct forms of the modals in italics.

a It's one of the greatest films ever made.
b I searched high and low for my wallet.
c The most important thing is to keep trying.
d I'm determined to leave school at 16.
e They're identical twins.
f This digital radio doesn't work properly.

1 ☐ I *could/couldn't* find it anywhere.
2 ☐ Nobody *can/can't* talk me out of it.
3 ☐ I *ought/ought not* to send it back.
4 ☐ You really *must/mustn't* see it.
5 ☐ Even their friends *can/can't* tell them apart.
6 ☐ You *should/shouldn't* never give up.

2 Rewrite the sentences in a–e without using *mustn't* and including the expressions in brackets.

a We mustn't wear jeans at this school. (allowed to)
We ....

b You mustn't swim in this part of the river. (prohibited)
Swimming ....

c We mustn't use a dictionary in the exam. (against the rules)
Using ....

d In the UK, children under 13 mustn't work. (against the law)
It ....

e In some train compartments, you mustn't use mobile phones. (forbidden)
The use ....

Grammar Extra

Modal verbs: permission and requests

3 Tick the modal verbs which can correctly complete sentences a–f. There may be more than one possible answer.

a These bags are rather heavy. .... you give me a hand, please?
Can ☐ Could ☐ May ☐ Would ☐

b I'm sorry, but you .... smoke in my house.
cannot ☐ could not ☐ may not ☐ would not ☐

c .... I borrow your car this weekend?
Can ☐ Could ☐ May ☐ Would ☐

d .... you mind keeping an eye on my bike while I'm in the shop?
Can ☐ Could ☐ May ☐ Would ☐

e I wonder if you .... tell me where the nearest post office is?
can ☐ could ☐ may ☐ would ☐

f You .... change channels, if you don't like this programme.
can ☐ could ☐ may ☐ would ☐

Listening

Part 1 Multiple choice

1 **Read the questions in the exam task in 3 and say which extracts (1–8) sentences a–h below probably come from.**

a I've always wanted to visit Tokyo. ☐

b And where are you travelling to? ☐

c The flight's very full, I'm afraid. ☐

d But the reality, according to this research, will be very different – and a lot dirtier. ☐

e No other car on the road today can make that claim. ☐

f When I booked the holiday, I was told that I'd have a sea view. ☐

g With my job, you spend most of your time on the road. ☐

h Of course, when I was a girl, there weren't any cars or buses in town. ☐

2 **Listen once to the recording in 3 and check your answers to 1. Then do the exam task in 3.**

3 **You will hear people talking in eight different situations. For questions 1–8 choose the best answer (A, B or C).**

1 You hear a woman complaining about her holiday. What aspect of the hotel is she unhappy with?
   A the staff
   B her accommodation
   C the facilities

2 You hear a ticket inspector talking to a passenger on a train. What has the passenger done?
   A He's lost his ticket.
   B He's passed his destination.
   C He's boarded the wrong train.

3 You hear an excerpt from a radio programme. What form of transport will **not** be used significantly more in 25 years' time, according to the programme?
   A cars
   B planes
   C bicycles

4 You hear two women imagining the trip of a lifetime. What do they agree about?
   A the length of the holiday
   B the method of transport
   C the first destination

5 You hear a woman remembering her childhood. How did she use to get to school?
   A on the handlebars of her brother's bike
   B on foot
   C by tram

6 You hear a man on a plane talking to one of the cabin crew. Why is he unhappy with his seat?
   A He doesn't like the person sitting next to him.
   B He'd prefer a seat by the aisle.
   C He's too close to the wing.

7 You hear a lorry-driver talking about other road-users. Which are the worst, in his opinion?
   A taxi drivers
   B minibus drivers
   C drivers of sport cars

8 You hear an advert for a new model of car. What is special about it?
   A The engine does not create any pollution.
   B The windscreen is unbreakable.
   C When the sun shines, the roof opens automatically.

Use of English

Part 4 Key word transformations

1 Complete each of sentences a–g with one of the conjunctions in the box. Use a dictionary to help you if necessary.

after as even though in case unless
whereas whether

a My brother is an experienced driver, ... he's only 19.
b Jack gazed out of the window of the train .... he ate his sandwich.
c We're going to travel by plane .... you like it or not.
d I'll be home by lunchtime .... the flight is delayed.
e You should carry your phone with you .... your car breaks down.
f The ferry is slower: it takes five hours, ... it only takes two hours by plane.
g They're planning to backpack around Europe .... they finish their exams.

2 For questions a–e, complete the second sentence so that it has a similar meaning to the first sentence, using the word given. Do not change the word given. You must use between two and five words, including the word given.

a If we don't get to the station in five minutes, we'll miss our train.
unless
We'll miss our train .... to the station in five minutes

b Her family moved to France and then she got a job as a flight attendant.
after
She got a job as a flight attendant .... to France.

c During the walk home from work, my dad always makes phone calls.
as
My dad always makes phone calls .... from work.

d You might lose your passport, so make a note of the number.
case
Make a note of your passport number .... it.

e In spite of the freezing weather, we had a great holiday in Canada.
even
We had a great holiday in Canada, ... was freezing.

Review Units 4–6

1 **Complete types of TV programmes a–e using the words in the box, then match them with extracts 1–5 below.**

bulletin	forecast	opera	programme	show

a chat .... ☐
b cookery .... ☐
c news .... ☐
d soap .... ☐
e weather .... ☐

1 *A hurricane has hit the southeast coast of the USA.*
2 *Tomorrow will be bright in the south.*
3 *Add the flour and mix well.*
4 *I'm sorry, but I'm in love with somebody else.*
5 *Today we'll be discussing love at first sight.*

2 **Underline any incorrect uses of simple and continuous tenses in sentences a–f. Tick the sentences that do not contain an error.**

a How many times have I been telling you not to leave the windows open?
b Are you considering going abroad to do your degree?
c I'm doubting that Suzie has been learning French for more than a few months.
d I'm not buying that book – it's costing too much!
e I imagine the house will be beautiful once you've finished all the work.
f I don't understand why you don't enjoy this meal – it's delicious!

3 **Complete sentences a–f with *a*, *an*, *the* or no article.**

a Fifty years ago, ... people couldn't have imagined how important .... computers would be today.
b Would you like to have .... dinner in .... garden this evening?
c My grandfather was .... tall man with .... dark hair.
d Jackson Pollock was .... artist who lived and died in .... USA.
e Could you stand by .... door while I take .... photo of you?
f .... Mount Etna is in .... Sicily, which is .... island in .... Mediterranean.

4 **Write the words in a–d in the correct order to make sentences expressing probability. Then number the sentences from 1 (least likely) to 4 (most likely).**

a will are chances the that rain it
.... ☐
b I'll there's that this no exam way pass
.... ☐
c before we'll it's that home midnight unlikely get
.... ☐
d later phone or sooner he's to bound
.... ☐

5 **Read the reported speech in a–f, then complete the equivalent direct speech.**

a The neighbours asked him not to tell anyone.
'............ anyone.'
b The police ordered him to put his hands on his head.
'............ head!'
c His friend asked him how to make curry .
'............ curry?'
d Jenny agreed to help him with his homework.
'............ homework.'
e The managing director advised her to apply for the job.
'............ job.'
f The kidnappers warned him not to contact the police.
'............ the police.'

6 **Complete sentences a–f by adding a prefix from the box. Use each prefix once.**

anti	mis	over	re	semi	under

a She felt ....dressed at the wedding wearing just jeans and a T-shirt.

b Nearly half a million people attended the ....war demonstration.

c The 2007 film *Flash Gordon* was a ....make of an earlier film.

d She failed the exam because she was ....confident and didn't bother to revise.

e Can you lend me some money? I must have ....placed my wallet.

f I grew up in an ordinary ....-detached house in the South.

7 **Complete gaps 1–7 in this advertisement for a car using the words in the box.**

boot	brakes	engine	ignition	roof
steering wheel	windscreen			

The new FT 150 has a powerful (1).................. designed to deliver maximum power with minimum pollution. It's certainly a hi-tech car. A new kind of (2).................. uses fingerprint recognition to start the car, rather than a traditional key. The audio system and satellite navigation can both be controlled without taking your hands off the (3).................., as can the automatic (4).................. which folds back at the flick of a switch and stores itself in the (5).................. in under 30 seconds. It's one of the safest cars on the market too. Not only is the (6).................. heated to ensure excellent visibility even in icy conditions, but the (7).................. are also designed to perform perfectly whatever the weather.

8 **For 1–6, choose the correct words in italics to complete the dialogue.**

Man	Excuse me. (1) *Could/Would* you mind telling me where the Museum of Modern Art is?
Woman	Not at all. It's in West Avenue, opposite the bus.
Man	(2) *Could/May* I walk there, do you think?
Woman	Yes, but it's about three kilometres.
Man	Maybe I (3) *must/ought to* get a taxi.
Woman	Or you (4) *could/should* get a bus. The stop is right here.
Man	Great! (5) *May/Would* I ask if you've been to the museum yourself?
Woman	Yes, I have. It's definitely worth a visit. You (6) *may/must* make sure you see the sculptures in the museum garden, too. They're beautiful.

9 **Circle the correct conjunctions to complete sentences a–e.**

a *As/Whereas* it's late, we should have dinner at the hotel.

b It's a good idea to photograph any valuable jewellery that you own *if/in case* it gets stolen.

c I really like Darren, *as though/even though* he's occasionally rude to me.

d We'll go walking in the hills, *unless/until* the weather's terrible tomorrow.

e *Since/While* you've been so well behaved, you can have an ice cream.

I get the message 7

Reading

Part 3 Multiple matching

1 Read the texts opposite about pioneers in the field of communications. Find out what each person invented.

a Gutenberg invented ....
b Braille invented ....
c Morse invented ....
d Bell invented ....

2 Read the texts again carefully. For questions 1–15, choose from the people (A–D). The people may be chosen more than once.

Which person
1 was born more than 500 years ago?
2 sufferered a terrible injury at a young age?
3 had another career before starting to invent?
4 was inspired by a miliary invention?
5 lived in the USA but was not born there?
6 personally obtained a patent?
7 tried hard to convince people of the importance of his invention?
8 nearly gave up the rights to his invention?
9 did not make much money from his invention?
10 helped to educate people in many countries?
11 developed his invention using something belonging to one of his parents?
12 developed his invention based on something he heard on a ship?
13 developed inventions to help combat a family member's disability?
14 had a difficult time during his education?
15 produced a book about his invention?

Pioneers

A Johannes Gutenberg

Johannes Gutenberg, who was born around the year 1400 in Germany, is widely regarded as the inventor of the modern printing press. Before about 1450, most books were written or copied by hand. This made them extremely time-consuming to produce and expensive to buy. But in 1455, Gutenberg developed a machine which could print multiple copies of the same book. These printed books were sold for 30 florins each, and although this represented three years' wages for an average office worker at the time, it was still considerably cheaper than a handwritten book. Today, there are 48 copies of Gutenberg's first book in existence. Two are at the British Museum and can be viewed online. Gutenberg did not achieve financial success as a result of his breakthrough – the rich at that time regarded printed books as inferior and preferred handwritten works – but his invention helped to spread knowledge across Europe and was a major factor in the Renaissance.

B Louis Braille

Born in France in 1809, Louis Braille became blind at the age of three after an accident in his father's workshop. When he was ten, he earned a place at a special school for blind children in Paris, one of the first institutions of its kind in the world. Although this saved Louis from the normal fate of the blind at that time – begging for money on the streets – life at the school was not easy or comfortable, and Braille was served bread and water. In 1821, Charles Barbier, a former soldier, visited the school and talked about a code that he'd invented which allowed soldiers to share information on the battlefield without speaking. The code used dots that could be felt with the fingertips. Impressed by this idea, Louis worked on his own code to help the blind read, using one of his father's tools to make the dots – ironically, the same kind of tool that had caused him to lose his sight twelve years earlier. The code that Louis invented has become standard throughout the world. The first book ever printed using Braille was a book Braille himself had written about his new system of writing.

C Samuel Morse

Samuel Morse, born in 1791 in Massachusetts, USA, started his career not as an inventor but as an artist. He had great artistic talent, and soon became well known for his portraits, but he also had a passion for new technology. In 1832, while travelling home by sea from Europe, he overheard a conversation about electromagnetism, and this gave him the idea for a new form of communication: the electric telegraph. Although other inventors had developed similar machines, Morse's worked better and he applied for, and got, the patent[1] in 1837. For the next five years, Morse tried to persuade politicians and businessmen in the USA to invest in a network of telegraph wires for sending messages between cities, but most of them did not believe such a system could ever work. And yet, a few years later, telegraph wires encircled the earth allowing instant messages to be sent from one continent to another.

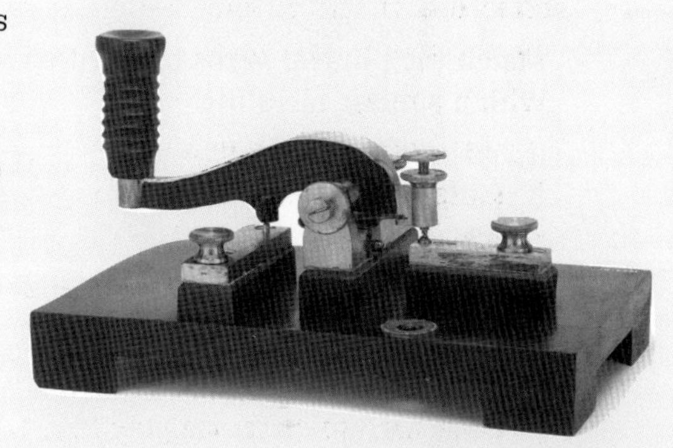

D Alexander Graham Bell

A pioneer in the field of telecommunications, Alexander Graham Bell was born in 1847 in Edinburgh, Scotland. He moved to Canada and then to the United States, settling in Boston, before beginning his career as an inventor. Perhaps because of his mother's hearing problems, Bell had a particular interest in the education of deaf people. This led him to invent the microphone and, in 1876, his 'electrical speech machine', which we now call a telephone. Bell was not the only inventor working in this field, but his lawyer managed to secure the all-important patent which gave Bell ownership of the idea. Bell and his partners tried to sell the patent to Western Union, a large communications company in the USA, for $100,000. The president of the company thought it was too much to pay. Two years later, he admitted to colleagues that if he could get the patent for $25 million, he would consider it a bargain. But by that time, Bell was not interested in selling and was already a rich man.

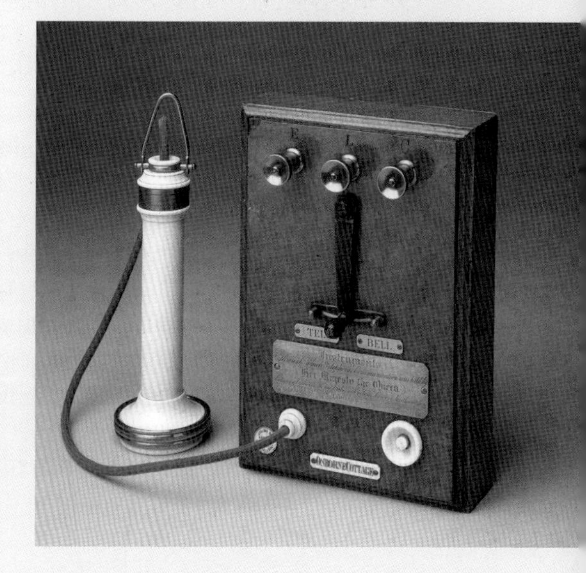

[1] patent = the official right to be the only person to make, use or sell a product or invention

Vocabulary

Phrasal verbs

1 **In sentences a–f mark where the particle in capitals goes. If two positions are possible, mark both, as in the example.**

Example *Can you pick ⋀ my jacket ⋀ from the cleaners? UP*

a I didn't want to let my parents by failing my exams. DOWN
b You've summed my opinion perfectly. UP
c The shopkeeper ran the thief, shouting. AFTER
d I came some interesting facts while researching my project. ACROSS
e They called the match because of the weather. OFF
f The president stood his deputy throughout the crisis. BY

2 **Match the phrasal verbs in 1 with a verb below with a similar meaning.**

a encounter ....
b support ....
c summarise ....
d disappoint ....
e chase ....
f cancel ....

3 **Rewrite the underlined parts of sentences a–f using a phrasal verb from the box. Put the object between the parts of the phrasal verb, if possible.**

ask for	bring up	bring up	carry on
cut off	turn on		

a Nobody knew why the dog suddenly attacked its owner.
b It is difficult for Hollywood stars to raise children in a normal environment.
c The phone company disconnected my grandmother because they claimed she hadn't paid her bill.
d We can continue this conversation when we meet tomorrow.
e The prisoner requested a newspaper.
f Lucy obviously didn't want to discuss the court case, so I didn't mention it.

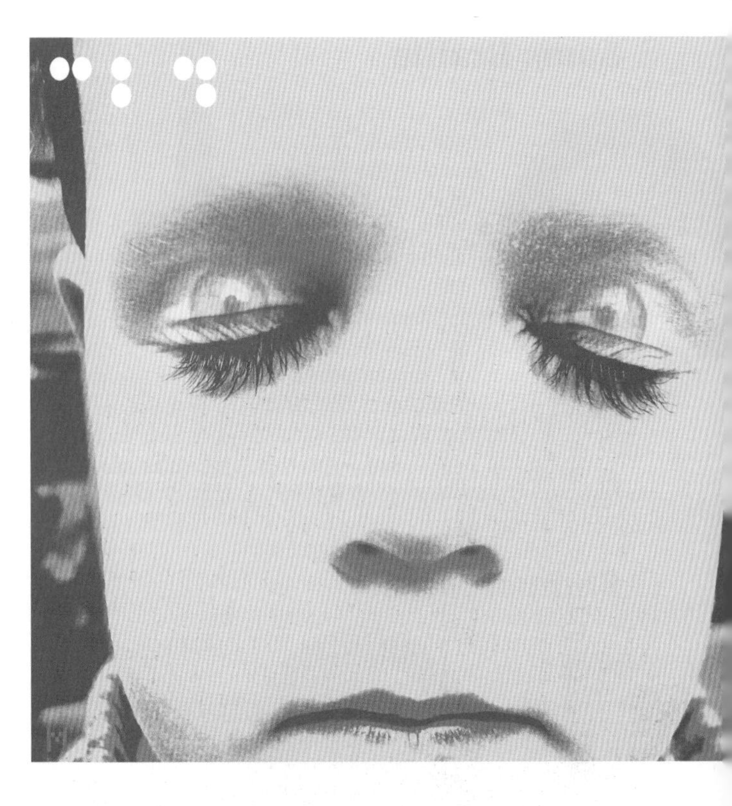

Body movements

4 **Tick the actions below which usually make a sound.**

a blink
b clap
c click your fingers
d duck
e gasp
f shiver
g sigh
h stamp
i wave

5 **Complete sentences a–e with verbs from 4 in an appropriate form.**

a As he stepped out of the cave, the bright sunlight made him ....
b The king .... his hands and immediately a servant entered.
c The cold night air made Jane .... as she walked home.
d Jeff threw the ball hard to Simon, but instead of catching it, he .... and the ball flew over his head.
e Louisa was sad to leave, but she said nothing; she just .... quietly to herself and .... goodbye.

Grammar

Passives

1 Read version A of the text, then complete version B with passive forms.

THE ROSETTA STONE

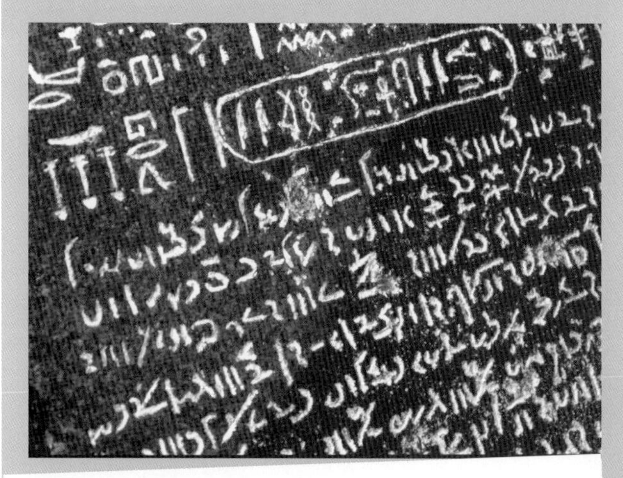

A Somebody discovered the Rosetta Stone in 1799 as French troops were building a fort in Egypt. It was a large stone which somebody had covered in writing about two thousand years earlier. They had written the text in three different scripts: hieroglyphic (picture writing), ancient Egyptian and ancient Greek. At the time when they found the stone, people had seen hieroplyphics on Pyramids and other ancient Egyptian monuments, but nobody could understand them. The Rosetta Stone provided the key. People compared the hieroglyphics with the other texts on the stone and gradually they deciphered them. Today, they display the Rosetta Stone in the British Museum in London.

B The Rosetta Stone (1) .... in 1799 as French troops were building a fort in Egypt. It was a large stone which (2) .... in writing about two thousand years earlier. The text (3) .... in three different scripts: hieroglyphic (picture writing), ancient Egyptian and ancient Greek. At the time when the stone (4) .... , hieroplyphics (5) .... on Pyramids and other ancient Egyptian monuments, but nobody could understand them. The Rosetta Stone provided the key. The hieroglyphics (6) .... with the other texts on the stone and gradually (7) .... Today, the Rosetta Stone (8) .... in the British Museum in London.

2 Complete sentences a–g with the correct passive infinitives of the verbs in the box.

attack cook lock sell release stop wear

a These shoes look brand new. They can't ....

b You can't eat mussels raw. They must ....

c If there's any more trouble in the crowd, the match should ....

d When I went back to the shop, the picture was no longer in the window. It must ....

e You shouldn't have left me alone in that part of the city at night. I might ....

f As soon as the prisoner was found not guilty, he should ....

g The burglars got in through the back door, which can't ....

3 Rewrite the sentences beginning with the words given, as in the example.

Example It is believed that water existed on Mars.
Water *is believed to have existed on Mars.*

a It was once thought that tomatoes were poisonous.
Tomatoes ....

b It is now known that the Black Death was brought to Europe by rats.
The Black Death ....

c It is believed that Archimedes was born around 287 BC.
Archimedes ....

d It is now thought that the dinosaurs were wiped out by a meteor impact.
The dinosaurs ....

e It was once believed that witches had the ability to change into cats.
Witches ....

Listening

Part 3 Multiple matching

1 You will hear five different people talking about their use of modern communications technology. For questions 1–5, choose from the list (A–F) the opinion each person expresses. Use the letters only once. There is one letter which you do not need to use.

1 Speaker 1 ....
2 Speaker 2 ....
3 Speaker 3 ....
4 Speaker 4 ....
5 Speaker 5 ....

A spends a lot more money on text messages than on voice calls
B feels that people should write more by hand
C doesn't think text messages are fast enough
D feels more at ease communicating with people online
E thinks the fact that you can be contacted at all times is stressful
F thinks that sending one personal email to lots of different people is lazy

2 Decide which word the speakers in 1 used in these sentences. Then listen again and check.

Speaker 1 I suppose I'm suspicious *at/of/with* technology in general.
Speaker 2 If you send enough messages, the bill really starts to add *in/over/up.*
Speaker 3 Emails are great for work, or for keeping *at/in/on* touch with people.
Speaker 4 I like to visit chat rooms whenever I'm *at/in/on* the Internet.
Speaker 5 Recently, I've completely switched *on/to/over* instant messaging.

Use of English

Part 1 Multiple-choice cloze

1 **Read the text below, ignoring the gaps. Which of conclusions a–c did the scientists reach about the horse's apparent ability to communicate with people?**

a They decided that Hans genuinely had the ability to do maths questions.
b They showed that Hans was not genuinely answering questions.
c They could not decide how Hans answered the questions.

2 **Read the text again carefully and for questions 1–12 decide which answer (A, B, C or D) best fits each gap.**

	A	B	C	D
0	A paid	B gained	(C) bought	D funded
1	A belonged	B had	C owned	D owed
2	A recognise	B realise	C suppose	D consider
3	A inform	B spend	C do	D tell
4	A claw	B hoof	C foot	D toes
5	A however	B but	C although	D despite
6	A asked	B told	C had	D got
7	A welcoming	B catching	C receiving	D picking
8	A good	B accurate	C even	D right
9	A relaxed	B relaxing	C resting	D restful
10	A denied	B rejected	C refused	D disagreed
11	A costing	B paying	C charging	D purchasing
12	A sensitive	B sensible	C sensational	D senseless

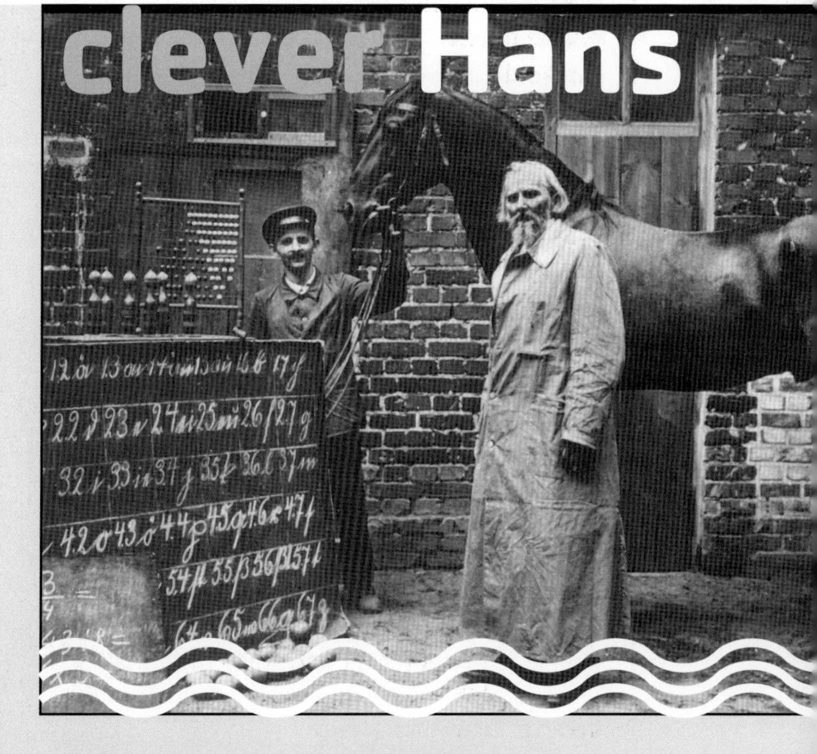

Hans the horse was (0) *bought* in 1900 by Wilhelm von Osten, a retired German schoolmaster, who was convinced that animals (1) .... an intelligence equal to that of humans. Von Osten taught the horse to (2) .... the numbers one to nine. In a short time, the horse could add, subtract, multiply, divide, (3) .... the time and keep track of the calendar. Von Osten would ask Hans, 'If the eighth day of the month comes on a Tuesday, what is the date of the following Friday?' Hans would answer by tapping his (4) .... Questions could be spoken or written on a blackboard.

'Clever Hans' became enormously popular and thousands of people came to see his demonstrations. Many scientists, (5) .... , had doubts about Hans' abilities, and a psychologist called Pfungst was asked to examine the case. In one test, Pfungst (6) .... the questioner write the question on the blackboard and then immediately leave the room. Unable to see the questioner or any other human, Clever Hans was unable to answer the question.

It became clear that the horse was (7) .... clues by watching people in the room. As the horse's taps approached the (8) .... answer, the questioner's body language and expression became more tense. When Hans made the final, 'correct' tap, the questioner automatically became more (9) .... Hans would notice this sudden change and would stop tapping.

Von Osten (10) .... to believe Pfungst's findings, and continued to show Hans around Germany, attracting large and enthusiastic crowds, but never (11) .... for admission. Although Pfungst had proved that Hans was not using intelligence to work out the answers, the episode demonstrated how (12) .... animals can be to human body language.

A matter of taste

8

Reading

Part 2 Gapped text

1 **Read the text opposite, ignoring the gaps, and find words that mean the same as a–g.**

a meeting (l. 1)
b introduction of a product for the first time (l. 8)
c gradually making unavailable (l. 17)
d admits (l. 34)
e in agreement with (l. 39)
f carried out (l. 48)
g without caring that they might harm other people (l. 68)

2 **Read the text again carefully, then match sentences A–H with gaps 1–7. There is one extra sentence.**

A However, at the end of last year, the company quietly took it off the menu, blaming a lack of demand for such healthy dishes.
B We know that people will report that 'Black Forest Double-Chocolate Cake' tastes better than 'Chocolate Cake', even when the cakes themselves are identical.
C Nevertheless, fast-food customers say they resent being told what to eat by self-righteous critics.
D There is no trace of lettuce or tomato or onion in the Stacker Quad, a fact trumpeted in the TV ads that accompanied the launch of the product in the United States.
E This phenomenon is known as 'unit bias' – the way we tend to think that whatever quantity a product is sold in must be the appropriate amount to consume.
F People tell researchers what they think they want to hear, or what the respondents want to believe about themselves.
G Perhaps you never set foot in fast-food restaurants, and you are feeling complacently immune to all this.
H It is worth recalling how strange these developments would have seemed just two years ago, when the fast-food backlash was at its height.

You do not forget your first encounter with a Burger King Stacker Quad. If you summon the nerve to order it, you'll be served with four beef patties, four slices of
5 cheese, and four strips of bacon in a bun. **[1]** The Stacker Quad may be extraordinary, but it is far from unique. Recent times have seen the launch – mainly in America – of a rash of products that the industry calls 'indulgent offerings':
10 foods marketed specifically on the basis of how much meat and cheese and how few annoying vegetables they contain. **[2]** Burger chains across the world, responding to alarming market research, began offering salads and fruit and fresh
15 juices. McDonald's launched the GoActive meal, which consisted of a salad and bottled water. It also began phasing out its supersized meals. The American burger restaurant Wendy's added a fresh-fruit bowl to its menu. **[3]** 'We listened to
20 consumers who said they wanted to eat fresh fruit,' a disarmingly honest spokesman told the New York Times, 'but apparently they lied.'

The industry's mistake, it seems, had been to listen to the market researchers instead of the
25 food psychologists. **[4]** But we know, thanks to recent psychological research, that people drink more than a third more fruit juice when they pour it into a short, wide glass instead of a narrow, tall one, and that people will eat more of a product
30 if it comes in a bigger package. **[5]** Above all, we know that just because people say they want to eat more healthily, it doesn't mean they really do want to.

Denny Marie Post, from Burger King, concedes
35 that the fast-food industry vastly overestimated the appeal of healthier product lines. 'Healthy eating is more a state of intention than it is of action,' she says. 'There is a very small percentage whose behaviour is consistent with their intentions. And
40 then there's a large percentage of people, and I include myself here, who wake up every

morning saying, "I'm going to be better today", but when it comes down to it and you're hungry and ready to eat ... then things are different.' **[6]** If so, you should take a look at the work of Andrew Geier, a psychologist at the University of Pennsylvania who recently conducted an experiment in which he placed a large bowl of sweets in the lobby of an apartment building. 'Eat your fill. Please use the spoon to serve yourself' read a sign he placed next to the bowl. He left it there for 10 days in a row, with, on alternate days, either a teaspoon or a large spoon that held a quarter of a cup of sweets. When they were using the bigger spoon, people on average took two thirds more sweets. **[7]** Yoghurt pots in France are about half as big as yoghurt pots in the US, Geier and his colleagues found, but the French do not buy twice as many pots of yoghurt. 'That's just the size they expect a yoghurt to be,' says Geier. The creeping expansion of portion sizes influences us all, unknowingly, inside fast-food restaurants and outside.

Many people believe that the fast-food corporations are cynically playing on our weaknesses in order to increase their profits. On the other hand, of course, you could argue that there is a refreshing honesty in products such as the Stacker Quad – it's a fatty pile of meat, and doesn't pretend otherwise.

EXTREME dining

Vocabulary

Word pairs

1 Join words in the first box with words in the second to make common word pairs. Make sure the words are in the correct order, then check your answers in a dictionary.

bread chairs chips forks pots salt

butter fish knives pans pepper table

a .... and ....
b .... and ....
c .... and ....
d .... and ....
e .... and ....
f .... and ....

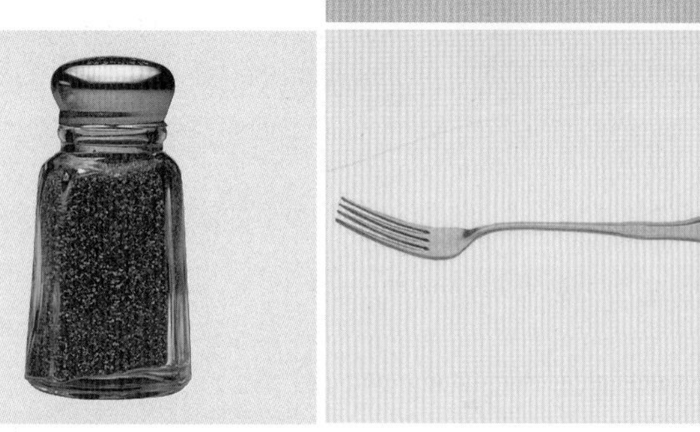

2 Complete word pairs a–h with *and*, *by*, *in* or *to*, then match them with definitions 1–8. The first one has been done as an example.

a side ....*by*.... side *3*
b go on .... on
c go from strength .... strength
d bit .... bit
e a heart .... heart
f more .... more
g all .... all
h face .... face

1 continue for a very long time
2 become increasingly successful
3 next to each other
4 with the other person present
5 gradually
6 a conversation about personal problems
7 increasingly
8 taking everything into account

3 Use the word pairs from 2 to complete a–h.

a Will you stop going .... about how busy you are? I'm getting really fed up with it.
b If you can't afford to pay off your debts in one go, you can pay them off .... over a number of years.
c The band is going .... They've had number one albums in three consecutive years.
d I felt a lot better after my .... with Becky. She was really sympathetic and understanding.
e I think it would be better if we put the fridge and freezer .... rather than one on top of the other.
f Dad is getting .... forgetful as he gets older.
g I prefer to discuss important issues .... rather than on the phone.
h I thought some of the acting was a bit wooden, but .... I enjoyed the play.

Grammar

Speculating about the present and past

1 **Match sentences a–f with replies 1–6, then complete them in an appropriate way. The first one has been done as an example.**

a He eats nothing but fast food.
b What's that smell?
c This chicken is very chewy.
d Dad never helps in the kitchen. He claims he can't cook.
e What herb is that in the pasta sauce?
f I can't cook dinner for ten people all on my own.

1 Oh, no! The sausages must be ...
2 It might be ...
3 Samantha might be able to ...
4 I wouldn't eat it. It can't be ...
5 He can't be ...
6 He must be able to ...

2 **Rewrite sentences a–f using** ***must (have), might (have)*** **or** ***can't (have).***

a I'm sure that Joe hasn't gone out. His shoes are here by the door.
.... His shoes are here by the door.

b I can possibly lend you some money.
....

c I'm sure there were over 100 people at the meeting.
....

d What a terrible draught! I'm sure one of the windows is open.
What a terrible draught! ....

e I'm sure the petrol tank isn't empty. I only filled it up two days ago.
.... I only filled it up two days ago.

f It's possible that Lucy was joking when she said that.
....

Grammar Extra

3 **Complete sentences a–e with** ***so*** **or** ***such.***

a The children were .... excited on the drive to the seaside that they couldn't keep still.
b I've never seen .... a beautiful sunset.
c I knew you'd say that. You're .... predictable!
d If he weren't .... mean, he'd have more friends.
e She's got .... lovely, dark eyes.

4 **Rewrite sentences a–e using the word given.**

a It was such bad weather that the tennis match was called off.
so
.... that the tennis match was called off.

b This is the best coffee I've ever tasted.
such
I've never ....
....

c The box of books was too heavy to lift by myself.
so
The box of books was ....
.... lift it by myself.

d He's so good at football that he could easily become a professional.
footballer
He's .... he could easily become a professional.

e It took us such a long time to get to the airport that we missed our flight.
so
It took .... to get to the airport that we missed our flight.

Listening

Part 3 Multiple matching

1 Match the words and phrases in 1–10 with the verbs they often follow (a–j).

a	stick by	1	a gym
b	go on	2	my principles
c	lose	3	my notice
d	make	4	weight
e	hand in	5	a decision
f	make	6	a cottage
g	work	7	an effort
h	live off	8	a diet
i	join	9	takeaways
j	rent	10	long hours

2 You will hear five different people talking about how they have changed their lifestyle. Match A–F with Speakers 1–5. There is one extra letter.

Speaker 1 ....

Speaker 2 ....

Speaker 3 ....

Speaker 4 ....

Speaker 5 ....

A has started to eat a lot more

B has changed their diet for health reasons

C has started taking more exercise

D has changed their diet for moral reasons

E has moved house

F has changed jobs

Use of English

Part 3 Word formation

1 **Complete the table with the missing parts of speech, using your dictionary to help you.**

	Verb	Noun (thing)	Adjective
a	support	....	....
b	....	attraction	....
c	....	....	enjoyable
d	....	offence	....
e	....	....	informative
f	admire	....	....
g	....	respect	....
h	....	....	imaginative

2 **Rewrite sentences a–g using a word related to the underlined word. All the answers are from 1 above.**

a I admire his ability to keep calm under pressure.
His ability to keep calm under pressure
....

b He gave me a lot of support when I lost my job.
He was very ....

c A lot of women find him attractive.
A lot of women are ....

d I was very offended by his remarks.
I found his ....

e Children have much more imagination than adults.
Children are much ....

f You should be more respectful towards your parents.
You should show ....

g He really enjoys listening to modern jazz.
He gets a lot of ....

3 **Read the text opposite, then complete each gap with a word formed from 1–10.**

0 essence
1 necessary
2 science
3 refuse
4 natural
5 develop
6 willing
7 reluctant
8 ill
9 basic
10 possible

THE JAM SANDWICH DIET

We all know that a balanced diet is 0 *essential* for our health and well-being, but do we worry (1) .... about what children eat? Schoolboy Craig Flatman has astonished (2) .... by surviving for 15 years on a diet of jam sandwiches. At first, Craig's (3) .... to eat any other kinds of food drove his mum to despair, but she soon realised that he wasn't just being difficult. When he tries other foods he is physically sick.

Most children (4) .... go through a phase of not eating well, so much so that 'faddy' eating is now recognised as a normal part of a child's (5) .... In a survey conducted by University College London, nearly 20 per cent of children under seven were described as 'food neophobic', meaning they are (6) .... to try new foods. For some children, for example those with food allergies, this (7) .... is a result of negative associations they have with food. In other cases it can be a demand for attention or sometimes it can follow an (8) .... In most cases it lasts for a few weeks or months. For a minority of children like Craig however, this faddy eating becomes a way of life.

Craig has undergone medical tests, which revealed that he is (9) .... healthy but that he hasn't got enough iron in his blood. Doctors say there's a (10) .... that he will become anaemic if he doesn't start eating fruit and vegetables. 'I know it's going to be difficult, but I can't carry on like this,' says Craig. 'I can't go through my adult life eating jam sandwiches, I need a new start.'

Going to extremes 9

Reading Part 1 Multiple choice

1 **Read the text opposite, about people who have cheated at sport, and find out in which countries these sportswomen were born.**

a Stella Walsh
b Rosie Ruiz
c Tonya Harding

2 **Read the text again carefully, then for questions 1–8, choose the answer (A, B, C or D) which you think best fits according to the text.**

1 According to the writer, why do sportspeople cheat?
A They can't perfect their techniques.
B They don't want to train any more.
C It's the only way to gain an advantage over fellow competitors.
D Famous athletes like Ben Johnson have cheated.

2 Stella Walsh represented Poland because she
A felt more Polish than American.
B couldn't become an American citizen.
C was very young when she moved to the USA.
D didn't like America.

3 How did Stella Walsh die?
A She died in a fire.
B She was shot while trying to rob a bank.
C She was accidentally shot.
D She died in her sleep.

4 Why were the race organisers suspicious when Ruiz won the marathon?
A She didn't seem hot and tired.
B She was sweating too much.
C It was such a fast time.
D She didn't take the winner's medal.

5 Who saw Ruiz during the race?
A nobody
B other runners
C the race officials
D some spectators, towards the end of the race

6 How many times did Tonya Harding win the US figure skating championships?
A none
B once
C twice
D three times

7 Nancy Kerrigan couldn't compete in the 1994 championships because
A she fell and injured her leg.
B someone attacked and injured her.
C she hurt her leg while practising.
D she hit her leg on something.

8 What happened to Harding?
A She was convicted along with her ex-husband.
B She started a criminal investigation.
C She denied all knowledge of the crime.
D She was no longer able to take part in amateur skating competitions.

Sports cheats

Some sportspeople are prepared to go to extraordinary lengths to win. They spend years training their bodies and perfecting their technique, only to discover that another sportsperson can perform better. And there's often nothing they can do about it – unless, that is, they cheat. Read the sports pages nowadays and you are bound sooner or later to see the words 'performance-enhancing drugs'. From the East German athletes of the seventies, to the Canadian sprinter Ben Johnson in the Seoul Olympics, to cyclists in the Tour de France – it seems that the words 'top athlete' and 'drugs' can't stay apart. However, drugs are not the weapon of choice for all sportspeople who seek to gain an edge over their opponents. Here are the stories of three athletes who have resorted to more unusual methods of cheating.

the sprinter

In the 1930s and 40s, Stella Walsh was one of the fastest women in the world. She was born Stanislawa Walasiewiczowna in Poland on 3rd April 1911. When she was two years old, her family emigrated to the US and settled in Cleveland, Ohio. At school and university she excelled at sprinting, but as she was unable to get American citizenship she represented Poland rather than the US at the Olympic Games. At the 1932 Games she won the gold medal in the 100 metres and four years later she won silver. Walsh continued to compete as an amateur until 1954, setting 20 world records and winning 41 Amateur Athletic Union titles in sprints, the long jump and the discus. In recognition of her achievements, she was inducted into the US Track and Field Hall of Fame in 1975. Tragically, she died five years later when she was caught in crossfire during an armed robbery in Cleveland. The autopsy surprised everyone by revealing that Walsh had the body of a man.

the marathon runner

In the Boston Marathon held on 21st April 1980, 23-year-old Rosie Ruiz, a Cuban-born runner from New York, crossed the finish line in the third fastest time ever recorded by a female competitor. The surprising thing was that when she went up to collect the winner's medal, the race officials noticed that was barely sweating. The organisers of the race immediately became suspicious and started an investigation. They examined videotapes of the race and noticed that she didn't appear on them until near the end of the race. What is more, the course officials could find no evidence of Ruiz passing checkpoints on the 26-mile route, and fellow competitors could not recall her taking part in the race. Ruiz insisted that she had run the entire race, but a few spectators eventually came forward and testified they had seen her join the race about a mile or half a mile from the finish line. It is assumed that she waited in the crowd and then sprinted to the finish line before proudly accepting the winner's medal.

the skater

It was a story of one woman's unhealthy thirst for stardom. Tonya Harding had a tough childhood in an unstable family in her home town of Portland, Oregon, USA. However, despite these difficulties she was by the end of the 1980s one of America's top figure skaters, and in 1989 she came close to winning the US figure skating championships. She finally achieved that goal in 1991, but she couldn't hold on to the title in the following year, and her career went into a decline. In 1994, Harding was in a heated battle with Nancy Kerrigan for the title she'd won three years before. But during practice for the championships, Kerrigan was hit in the leg and injured by a mysterious assailant. She had to pull out of the competition, and Harding was victorious again. However, Harding soon found herself in the middle of a criminal investigation into the attack on Kerrigan. Her ex-husband Jeff Gillooly was convicted of the crime but at his trial he claimed that Harding had been involved, which she later admitted was true, although she was never brought before a court. Harding was subsequently stripped of her national title and banned from amateur skating.

Vocabulary

Describing weather

1 Match a–d with definitions 1–4.

a gale ....
b blizzard ....
c heatwave ....
d downpour ....

1 period of very hot weather
2 very strong wind
3 sudden, heavy rain
4 severe snowstorm

2 Complete sentences a–d with words from 1.

a The meteorological office is predicting a .... next week. Temperatures are expected to reach 35°C.
b Yesterday's match was abandoned because of a sudden .... which flooded the pitch.
c Scores of trees were blown down in the .... that swept across Britain last night.
d We were trapped for eight hours in our car during the .... Eventually we were dug out by the emergency services.

3 Circle the word that has the strongest meaning in each pair a–f, using your dictionary to help you. Then complete the 'neutral' words in the middle.

a	chilly	c....................	freezing
b	soaking	w....................	damp
c	hazy	m....................	foggy
d	breeze	w....................	gale
e	downpour	r....................	shower
f	warm	h....................	scorching

4 Use the information in the dictionary entries to complete sentences a–f.

blus·tery /ˈblʌstəri/ *adj.* (of weather) with strong winds: ***blustery winds/conditions*** ◇ *The day was cold and blustery.*

dense /dens/ *adj.* (**dens·er**, **dens·est**) **1** containing a lot of people, things, plants, etc. with little space between them: *a **dense crowd/forest*** ◇ *areas of dense population* **2** difficult to see through SYN THICK: ***dense fog/smoke/fumes*** **3** (*informal*) stupid: *How can you be so dense?* **4** difficult to understand because it contains a lot of information: *a dense piece of writing* **5** (*technical*) heavy in relation to its size: *Less dense substances move upwards to form a crust.* ▶ **dense·ly** *adv.*: *a **densely populated** area* ◇ ***densely covered/packed***

gen·tle 0‒ /ˈdʒentl/ *adj.* (**gent·ler** /ˈdʒentlə(r)/ **gent·lest** /ˈdʒentlɪst/)
1 calm and kind; doing things in a quiet and careful way: *a quiet and gentle man* ◇ *a gentle voice/laugh/touch* ◇ *She was the gentlest of nurses.* ◇ *He lived in a gentler age than ours.* ◇ *Be gentle with her!* ◇ *She agreed to come, after a little **gentle persuasion**.* ◇ *He looks scary but he's really a **gentle giant**.* **2** (of weather, temperature, etc.) not strong or extreme: *a gentle breeze* ◇ *the gentle swell of the sea* ◇ *Cook over a gentle heat.* **3** having only a small effect; not strong or violent: *We went for a gentle stroll.* ◇ *a little **gentle exercise*** ◇ *This soap is very gentle on the hands.* **4** not steep or sharp: *a **gentle slope/curve/angle***—see also GENTLY ▶ **gentle·ness** /ˈdʒentlnəs/ *noun* [U]

mild 0‒ /maɪld/ *adj., noun*
■ ***adj.*** (**mild·er**, **mild·est**) **1** not severe or strong: *a **mild form** of the disease* ◇ *a **mild punishment/criticism*** ◇ *It's safe to take a mild sedative.* ◇ *Use a soap that is mild on the skin.* **2** (of weather) not very cold, and therefore pleasant: *the mildest winter since records began* ◇ *a mild climate*—compare HARD **3** (of feelings) not great or extreme SYN SLIGHT: ***mild irritation/amusement/disapproval*** ◇ *She looked at him in mild surprise.* **4** (of people or their behaviour) gentle and kind; not usually getting angry or violent SYN EQUABLE: *a mild woman, who never shouted* **5** (of a flavour) not strong, spicy or bitter: *a mild curry* ◇ *mild cheese* OPP HOT ▶ **mild·ness** *noun* [U]: *the mildness of a sunny spring day* ◇ *her mildness of manner*
■ ***noun*** [U] (*BrE*) a type of dark beer with a mild flavour: *Two pints of mild, please.*—compare BITTER

▶ **stif·ling** /ˈstaɪflɪŋ/ *adj.*: *a stifling room* ◇ ***'It's stifling** in here—can we open a window?'* ◇ *At 25, she found family life stifling.*

tor·ren·tial /təˈrenʃl/ *adj.* (of rain) falling in large amounts

Oxford Advanced Learner's Dictionary, 7th edition

a .... fog reduced visibility to 30 metres and made driving conditions very difficult.
b .... rain and high winds have recently caused widespread flooding in coastal regions.
c A .... wind made it very difficult to play tennis, as it blew the ball in all directions.
d The flags on the hotel fluttered in the .... breeze.
e The house is .... Let's open some windows.
f According to scientists, the .... wet winters are caused by global warming.

Grammar

Relative clauses

1 **Rewrite sentences a–e adding the information in brackets in an appropriate place. Use *who* or *which*, add commas where necessary, and make any other necessary changes.**

a *Friends* starts in five minutes. (It is my favourite sitcom.)

b The tall blond woman is Gary's girlfriend. (You were talking to her at the party.)

c Can you give me back the CDs? (You borrowed them about three weeks ago.)

d A local man has won the lottery. (We happen to know him.)

e Ranulph Twisleton-Wykeham Fiennes has just walked round the Arctic Circle. (was the first man to visit both Poles by land)

2 **Read a–e in 1 again and put brackets round the relative pronouns which can be omitted.**

3 **Complete sentences a–e using phrases 1–5 and *who, which, when, whose* or *where*.**

a I really like the hotel ...

b My brother, ...

c The woman ...

d That was the moment ...

e My wife hated the dress ...

1 you met at Christmas, has just got divorced.

2 it all became clear to me.

3 we stayed last year.

4 I bought for her birthday.

5 purse I found in the street turned out to be my neighbour.

4 **Tick the sentences in 3 which contain a defining relative clause, and say in which ones the relative pronoun can be omitted.**

Grammar Extra

5 **Rewrite sentences a–f using a present participle (*-ing*) clause or a past participle (*-ed*) clause.**

a The tall man who is standing next to the gate is my neighbour.

b To make the shelves I need four pieces of wood that measure 1.5 m by 20 cm.

c The youth who was attacked last night in the town centre is still in hospital.

d You can only eat food which has been bought in the canteen.

e Commuting is no fun for people who work in London.

f I'd like to own the house that faces the entrance to the park.

6 **Join the pairs of sentences in a–e using a participle clause.**

a That's my cousin. He's talking to Jenny.

b They live in a big house. It's made entirely of wood.

c Let's follow the path. It runs across the valley.

d I saw a man at the station. He tried to get on the train without a ticket.

e Do you recognise the man? He was seen stealing a car.

Listening

Part 2 Sentence completion

1 Listen to an extract from a radio programme about the climber Annabelle Bond, and say whether sentences a–e are true or false.

a It took her about a year to climb the seven mountains.

b Only four men have climbed the peaks faster than Annabelle.

c Annabelle always wanted to be a marathon runner.

d She raised £8,500 for a cancer charity.

e She plans to do more climbing in the near future.

2 Listen again and complete sentences 1–10.

1 The mountains Annabelle climbed are on seven different ....

2 Annabelle's father works for a ....

3 Annabelle's .... was also a climber.

4 While working as an estate agent, Annabelle had to train between .... with clients.

5 When she visited Everest base camp she was impressed with the magnificent ....

6 Two people who joined their group .... while climbing down Everest.

7 It was difficult to remain .... because of the limited diet.

8 She was accompanied on the climbs by .... from an adventure company.

9 During her year-long adventure she mostly lived in ....

10 Annabelle is getting a lot of work as a celebrity ....

Use of English

Part 4 Key word transformations

1 **Complete expressions a–i with *eyes*, *heart* or *mind*, then match them with definitions 1–9.**

a cross your ....
b make up your ....
c have in ....
d catch your ....
e be up to your .... in sth
f not see .... to ....
g set your .... on sth
h break your ....
i your .... sinks

1 be thinking of
2 occur to you
3 reach a decision
4 be very busy with
5 attract your attention
6 not have the same opinion
7 feel very discouraged
8 want very much
9 make you very unhappy

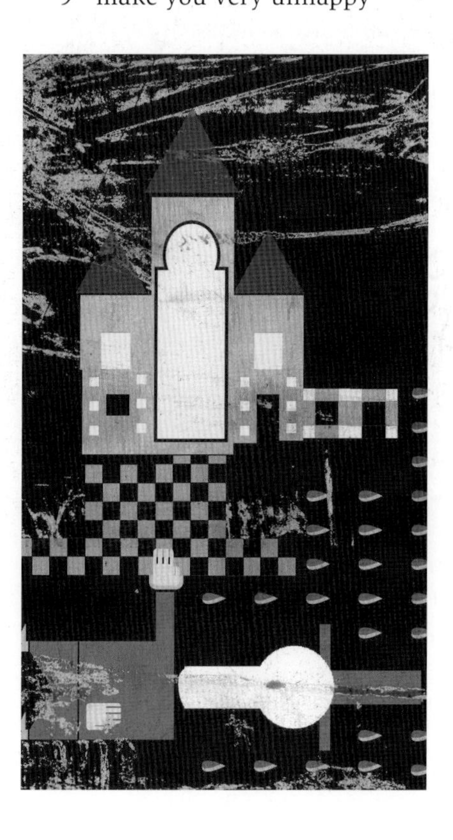

2 **For questions a–i, complete the second sentence so that it has a similar meaning to the first sentence, using the word given. Do not change the word given. You must use between two and five words, including the word given.**

a The restaurant was very busy so it was difficult to attract the waitress' attention.
eye
The restaurant was very busy so it was difficult to ....

b What were you thinking of when you suggested we go away this weekend?
mind
What .... when you suggested we go away this weekend?

c Harry really wants a holiday in Greece when he's finished his exams.
heart
Harry .... a holiday in Greece when he's finished his exams.

d Fred's very busy with work this week. He's hardly got a moment to spare.
eyes
Fred's .... in work this week. He's hardly got a moment to spare.

e Sandra was really upset when Danny broke off the engagement.
heart
It .... when Danny broke off the engagement.

f It never occurred to me that Jason would be offended.
mind
It .... that Jason would be offended.

g I couldn't decide whether to take a gap year or go straight to college.
mind
I couldn't .... whether to take a gap year or go straight to college.

h The goalkeeper felt really discouraged when he let in the third goal.
heart
The .... when he let in the third goal.

i Don and Joy agree on most things except for music.
eye
Don and Joy .... on most things except for music.

Review Units 7–9

1 Rewrite sentences a–f using the phrasal verbs given in capitals in the correct form.

a My parents supported me during the court case.
STAND BY

....

b The strike was cancelled when the management increased its pay offer.
CALL OFF

....

c At the end of the meeting Dave summarised what they had agreed.
SUM UP

....

d Dogs love chasing balls or sticks.
RUN AFTER

....

e Their father always collects the children from school.
PICK UP

....

f Wendy felt angry and disappointed.
LET DOWN

....

2 Choose the correct verb in italics to complete a–e.

a It's rude to *click/clap* your fingers to draw somebody's attention.

b We *stamped/shivered* our feet in the snow to keep warm.

c Robert *sighed/gasped* in astonishment when he heard the news.

d There's a man in the sea *waving/ducking* his arms. I think he needs help.

e He showed no surprise when I told him I was resigning. He didn't even *blink/sigh*.

3 Rewrite a–f with the particle belonging to the phrasal verb in the correct place.

a Carry the good work you are doing on.

b He called the waiter and asked some bread for.

c I don't know why Catherine suddenly turned me on and started yelling.

d My sister and I were brought in a small village up.

e The phone company will cut off you if you don't pay your bill.

f Joe brought the question of pay at the meeting with his manager up.

4 Rewrite sentences a–f using a passive construction. If two constructions are possible, write both.

a In the past people thought that the world was flat.

b They gave my grandfather a gold watch when he retired.

c The teacher told me to hand in my homework by Friday.

d The police stopped and searched the two boys.

e Everyone expected last year's champion to win Wimbledon.

f People say that the house is haunted.

5 Use the words below to complete word pairs in a–g.

all	face	heart	more	on	side	strength

a Jess and I had a .... to .... and she told me all about the problems she's been having at home.

b George went .... and .... about how Robin had upset him.

c .... and .... scientists are warning of the dangers of global warming.

d Shares in pharmaceutical companies are going from .... to ....

e .... in .... the school basketball team performed very well, even though they didn't win the match.

f Coming .... to .... with a grizzly bear was a terrifying experience.

g Stand .... by .... and we'll see which one of you is taller.

6 **Complete sentences a–f with *so* or *such* and other appropriate words.**

a The kids were having .... time that they didn't want to come home.

b It was .... that we had to put on the air-conditioning.

c Dad drove .... that we arrived at grandad's an hour earlier than expected.

d It was .... film that I fell asleep half way through.

e We stayed in .... hotel that we've booked to stay there again next year.

f This exercise was .... that I finished it in less than a minute.

7 **Complete the nouns and adjectives below, then use some of them to complete sentences a–e.**

noun	**adjective**
attract....................	attract....................
enjoy....................	enjoy....................
inform....................	inform....................
admir....................	admir....................
imagin....................	imagin....................

a He's a very intelligent boy but he lacks ....

b The article wasn't very .... so I didn't learn anything new from it.

c I don't do any sport myself, but I get lot of .... from watching it on TV.

d His willingness to help even total strangers is ....

e I don't understand the .... of city life. I much prefer living in the country.

8 **Complete sentences a–f with the verbs below in the present or past participle form.**

call injure make sit study walk

a Maria has got a son .... history at college.

b The people .... in the accident were taken to hospital.

c The shops are full of goods .... in China.

d The man .... in the deckchair is my cousin.

e Sue did a drawing of a man .... down the street.

f I've got a cat .... Thomas.

9 **For a–i, add verbs in the correct form to complete the expressions with *eye, heart* and *mind*.**

a It didn't .... my mind that he would object to you coming to London with us.

b I .... his eye but he didn't acknowledge me so I don't think he remembers me.

c I wish you'd .... your mind which hat you're going to wear.

d I'm not surprised they've fallen out. They don't .... eye to eye on anything.

e It .... my heart to see her so upset.

f 'Shall we do something exciting this weekend?' 'What did you .... in mind?'

g Sandra has .... her heart on a career in advertising.

h My heart .... when I saw how much work there was to do.

i John .... up to his eyes in revision for his exams.

10 **Read the definitions in a–l and write the appropriate adjectives and nouns.**

a very cold ....

b slightly cold ....

c very wet ....

d slightly wet ....

e very misty ....

f slightly misty ....

g very hot ....

h a little hot ....

i a very strong wind ....

j a gentle wind ....

k very heavy rain ....

l short period of rain ....

All in the mind

Reading

Part 2 Gapped text

1 **Read the text opposite, ignoring the gaps, and say which of methods for remembering information (a–f) it mentions.**

a divide the information into small sections
b link the information to a picture in your mind
c write the information down several times
d record the information and listen to it
e visualise different rooms of a building with information in each
f work in pairs and test each other

2 **Read the text again carefully, then choose from the sentences A–H the one which fits each gap (1–7). There is one extra sentence which you do not need to use.**

A These linked meanings can then form a story to help remember a really long sequence.
B It avoids wasting time learning the same information twice, and is also a good way of keeping your mind focussed on the task.
C This is because they have invented a personal meaning for each one.
D These will be easier to memorise than individual digits because there are fewer of them.
E Nevertheless, an improved memory is certainly very valuable to people involved in academic study.
F To recall the names later, you simply follow the same route in your mind.
G The same thing happens with spelling: most people repeat the same mistakes.
H For less obvious names, you'll have to get more creative.

Memory isn't like a muscle, something specific you can exercise. It's a way of organising information in your brain. So to improve your memory, you need to change and re-organise the way you think and this will help to support how your memory works.

Short-term memory is limited, and most people can only remember about seven items (numbers, names, objects, etc.) at a time. So when given a string of numbers to remember such as 123957001969, break it into chunks: 12 39 57 00 19 69 or even 1239 5700 1969. (1) .... The chunks will be even more memorable if you can attach a meaning to some or all of them. For example, you might be able to link them to the age of someone you know, an address or a famous date (e.g. 1969, the first moon landing). (2) ....

Another technique for memorising information relies on images. A classic way of remembering a person's name is to try and imagine it (or something associated to it) on the person's face. This is easy if you meet John Bridge: just imagine a bridge on his face. (3) .... Psychologists have found that the more unusual and vivid the image is, the better it works.

In order to improve your ability to memorise random information, look for meaning in everything – especially if you can refer it back to yourself. The human mind has a particular fondness for meaning. A sequence of playing cards is difficult to remember because the cards are essentially meaningless. And yet, some people have trained themselves to memorise the precise order of every card in a pack, and it only takes them a few minutes to do it. (4) ....

Make a mistake whilst learning something for the first time and you're more likely to make the same mistake again. But get it right from the start and it'll stick. This is called error-free learning. For instance, if you cycle to somebody's house for the first time and you take a wrong turning, it is quite common that you will repeat that mistake next time you go. This is because, when you repeat the journey, you recognise the route and the

Improve your memory

landmarks, and your brain will carry on misguiding you until you realise that you are just remembering the things you did wrong last time! It's not that your memory is poor but that it's misleading you. (5) .... So if you're 45 learning something new, cut out all distractions; this will help you learn it correctly first time.

In general, it is often better to test yourself on something you've learned than to keep re-learning it. This is because while testing yourself, you can reflect on your progress, 50 check how well you have learnt things, and fill in the gaps rather than re-learn everything again. (6) .... This applies, for example, when you are learning vocabulary in a foreign language.

And finally, there is an excellent technique for 55 remembering facts, called the 'Roman Room' method. It's a particularly good way of remembering a sequence of related information such as a list of names, and it works like this. Choose a place you know well – such as your home – and take a mental walk through the 60 rooms. Then, put the names from your list one by one into the rooms. Suppose you want to remember the names of your friend's brothers and sisters in order of age. Visualise Harry, the eldest, in your front room, then Sally the second in the back room. Molly, the third 65 oldest, is in the kitchen ... and so on. (7) .... It seems a strange way of remembering, but with practice it is very successful. It works because you are attaching new information to something which is already very familiar and easy to recall.

Vocabulary

Emotions and mental states

1 Put the words below into two groups, depending on whether they are generally considered positive or negative.

anxious cheerful contented depressed enthusiastic frustrated grateful nervous

positive	*negative*

2 Choose the best word (A, B or C) to complete sentences 1–6.

1 Although Suzie had revised thoroughly for the exam, she still felt .... as she turned over the paper.
A nervous B cheerful C enthusiastic

2 I'd like to say how .... I am for all the help you've given me.
A cheerful B frustrated C grateful

3 After lunch, we stretched out on the grass and closed our eyes, feeling warm and .... in the sunshine.
A anxious B contented C enthusiastic

4 Rationally, I know that flying is safe, but I still feel very .... during take-off and landing.
A anxious B depressed C grateful

5 When the burglars couldn't force the back door open, they became .... and smashed a window instead.
A nervous B enthusiastic C frustrated

6 Considering all the problems my sister has had, it's amazing that she's remained so ....
A cheerful B depressed C grateful

3 Complete the abstract nouns in the chart, using a dictionary to help you if necessary.

adjective	abstract noun
anxious	....................ty
nervous	....................ness
cheerful	....................ness
contented	....................ment
depressed	....................ion
enthusiastic	....................sm
frustrated	....................ion
grateful	....................tude

4 Form abstract nouns from adjectives 1–6, then complete a–f with the appropriate noun or adjective. Use a dictionary to help you if necessary.

1 confused ....
2 furious ....
3 miserable ....
4 excited ....
5 guilty ....
6 thrilled ....

a Our hotel was so bad that our holiday turned into two weeks of ....

b The release of a new *Star Trek* film always causes great .... among science fiction fans.

c She couldn't help feeling .... about what had happened, even though it wasn't her fault.

d It's important to explain the rules carefully now, to avoid any .... later.

e We've spent a year designing these clothes, and we're really .... with the result. They're great!

f Cancelling the concert at the last minute produced a(n) .... reaction from fans, who sent angry emails to the band's website.

Grammar

Comparatives and superlatives

1 **Find one mistake in each sentence a–h, then rewrite the sentence correctly.**

a The older I get, more I know.
b She's one of the nicest students of the class.
c London isn't as crowded than Tokyo.
d Last night's meal was more expensive that we had imagined.
e They say that the simplest things in life are the more important.
f That was probably the less scary horror film I've ever seen.
g The more hard I work, the less time I have for relaxation.
h Brandon is one of the kindest and generous people I've ever met.

2 **Rephrase the information in a–e using a comparative form of the adjective or adverb in brackets.**

Example Julie gets up at 6.00 am; Robert gets up at 7.30 am. (EARLY)
Julie gets up earlier than Robert.
OR Robert doesn't get up as early as Julie does.

a Freddie goes to the bank three times a week; Simon goes once a week. (often)

....

b Gail spends 30 minutes in the shower every day; Kevin spends 10 minutes in the shower. (long)

....

c A Porsche 911 GT3 costs £80,000; a Ferrari 599 GTB costs £180,000. (expensive)

....

d Lucy got 75 per cent in her Maths exam; Anna got 80 per cent. (well)

....

e Ben drives 36 km to work every day; Sandra drives 48km to work every day. (far)

....

3 **Rewrite sentences a–e to include the superlative form of the underlined adjective.**

Example You've never written an essay as good as this one.
This is the best essay you've ever written.

a Nobody can remember seeing a more exciting film than this one.
b You can't buy a more effective cleaner than Shine-X.
c We've never had a worse meal in a restaurant than this one.
d In my opinion, no actress in the world is more beautiful than Salma Hayek.
e I've never met a less arrogant person than your brother.

4 **Complete gaps 1–6 in the advertisement, using suitable comparative or superlative forms of the words below. Add any other necessary words.**

easy expensive fast late soon successful

Learn a language in 2 weeks

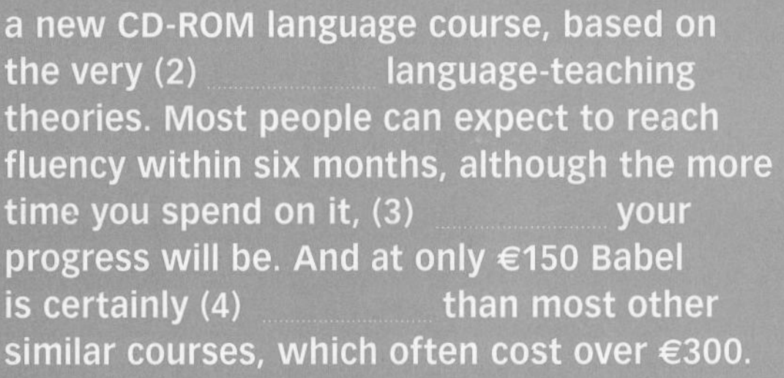

There has never been an (1) .... to learn a new language! Just spend an hour a day following Babel, a new CD-ROM language course, based on the very (2) .... language-teaching theories. Most people can expect to reach fluency within six months, although the more time you spend on it, (3) .... your progress will be. And at only €150 Babel is certainly (4) .... than most other similar courses, which often cost over €300.

Apply online for Babel, the language course described as '(5) .... method to have been invented in the past decade, judging by its results'. And remember, we're offering a 10% discount for the first 1,00 orders, so (6) .... you apply, the better your chance of paying less!

Listening

Part 3 Multiple matching

1 You will hear five different people talking about a vivid memory from childhood. Listen once and say how old each speaker is at the time of the event.

Speaker 1 ....

Speaker 2 ....

Speaker 3 ....

Speaker 4 ....

Speaker 5 ....

2 Listen again. For questions 1–5, choose from the list (A–F) the event that each person recalls. Use the letters only once. There is one extra letter which you do not need to use.

1 Speaker 1 ....

2 Speaker 2 ....

3 Speaker 3 ....

4 Speaker 4 ....

5 Speaker 5 ....

A getting lost in a crowd

B seeing an argument at home

C arguing with an elder sister

D breaking down on a major road

E moving to a new town

F being disappointed by a present

Use of English

Part 3 Word formation

1 Circle the word endings which are not common endings for adjectives, and say which other part of speech they usually indicate.

–able –al –ed –ness –tion –ful

2 Read the text opposite quickly, ignoring the gaps, and choose the best summary, a, b or c.

a A man proved on TV that he had special psychic abilities, even though people were sceptical.

b A man initially claimed to have special psychic abilities but later admitted that he had faked them.

c A man started a martial arts school for young students with special psychic abilities.

3 Read the text again carefully and decide which part of speech, a or b, is needed to complete each gap. There is an example at the beginning.

	a		b	
0	a adjective	☐	b noun	☑
1	a adjective	☐	b verb	☐
2	a adverb	☐	b noun	☐
3	a adjective	☐	b adverb	☐
4	a adjective	☐	b adverb	☐
5	a noun	☐	b adjective	☐
6	a adjective	☐	b verb	☐
7	a adjective	☐	b noun	☐
8	a adjective	☐	b verb	☐
9	a adverb	☐	b noun	☐
10	a adjective	☐	b adverb	☐

4 Complete the text with words formed from 1–10.

0 demonstrate
1 nation
2 able
3 success
4 natural
5 convince
6 sceptic
7 perform
8 able
9 fail
10 abrupt

A real page-turner?

In 1981, a man who claimed to have special psychic powers amazed TV audiences across the US with a simple (0) *demonstration*: using only the power of his mind, James Hydrick turned over the pages of a book. Later, on the same show, he made a pencil spin around without touching it. Hydrick became a (1) .... celebrity overnight, and ordinary people in the street started discussing 'telekinesis' – the (2) .... to move physical objects using only your mind.

Hydrick's career took off, and in addition to his TV appearances, he also became a (3) .... martial arts teacher. He even claimed that he could pass on his special gift of telekinesis to his young students. (4) .... , there were hundreds of youngsters who were desperate to learn, and happy to pay for lessons.

Unfortunately for Hydrick, not everybody was entirely (5) .... James Randi, an American magician, was publicly (6) .... about Hydrick's claims and insisted that his 'paranormal' powers were really just magic tricks. When Randi and Hydrick appeared on a TV show together, Randi placed small, very light pieces of plastic around the book just before Hydrick attempted his (7) .... Hydrick's paranormal powers deserted him, and he was (8) .... to turn even a single page. Although he invented a complicated excuse, the real reason for his (9) .... was simple: he could only turn the pages by blowing air from his mouth, and he couldn't do this without blowing away all the pieces of plastic and in the process revealing his secret. Hydrick's career ended (10) .... , and he later confessed to a newspaper that he had never possessed any special powers.

Man and machine 11

Reading

Part 1 Multiple choice

1 **Read the text opposite quickly to find out what slightly unusual thing the author does.**

a He repairs other people's electrical goods when they break.

b He repairs battery-operated toys for children.

c He tries to repair his own electrical goods when they break.

2 **Read the text again carefully and for questions 1–8, choose the answer (A, B, C or D) which you think fits best according to the text.**

1 In what way is William Painter associated with the disposable culture?
   A He invented a type of bottle top which could not be reused.
   B He sold drinks in bottles which had to be thrown away.
   C He invented the disposable razor.
   D He refused to refill bottles when people returned them.

2 In what sense are fridges and TVs disposable?
   A It is not possible to recycle electrical goods.
   B They are not worth repairing because the cost is too high.
   C You can buy disposable versions of them.
   D They are much cheaper than they used to be.

3 People often feel bad about throwing away electrical items because
   A they cost a lot of money to replace.
   B they know they could easily find somebody to repair them.
   C they feel they should be reducing the amount of rubbish they produce.
   D they know that disposable items are just a fashion.

4 The situation with disposable goods is made worse by the fact that
   A most people do not understand how electrical goods work.
   B the number of electrical goods in the home is increasing.
   C some electrical goods are faulty and get very hot when they're plugged in.
   D most electrical goods are made entirely of plastic.

5 If your bread-making machine breaks,
   A you have no chance of finding anyone to fix it.
   B you'll have to replace it with a better one.
   C you'll insist on having it repaired, unless you're quite eccentric.
   D you have a chance of finding somebody to fix it, if you keep trying.

6 It can't do any harm to try repairing things yourself because
   A they aren't worth much money once they're broken.
   B it's always easy to work out what the fault is.
   C you are sure to learn a lot by taking them apart.
   D they were badly made in the first place.

7 The author's advice about microwaves is that
   A it's better not to mention them in conversation.
   B repairing them takes a long time.
   C you have to be very careful if you try repairing them.
   D it's better not to try fixing them yourself.

8 Repairing appliances yourself is made easier by the fact that
   A you can get instructions from helpful repairmen.
   B most repairs can be done by the average consumer.
   C you can find advice and spare parts online.
   D you can use a computer to find out what the problem is.

ON THE MEND

The disposable culture started small. In 1892 William Painter, founder of the Baltimore Bottle Seal Company, patented the bottle cap. The bottles were returned and refilled, but the bottle caps were thrown away. They only worked once. Painter's chief salesman at the time was called Mr Gillette, who went on to apply the same principle to his own invention, the disposable razor blade. Today almost everything has its disposable version – cameras, contact lenses, barbecues – but the concept has been taken a step further. For economic reasons, most of the electrical equipment that we buy for the home is effectively disposable. This is because it is usually cheaper to replace them than to mend them. This applies not just to radios and toasters, but also to fridges, televisions and dishwashers. We now live in a disposable culture.

Most people feel uncomfortable about this new trend. We know we should be reducing the amount of waste we produce and recycling as much as possible – although despite all our efforts, landfill continues to increase. It's hard to slip a CD player into the bottom of the rubbish these days without feeling guilty, especially if you suspect that all it needs is a simple repair. But who fixes that sort of thing these days? And how much would they charge you?

Not only are we throwing more away these days, but also, modern life seems filled with new appliances – set-top boxes, modems, routers … . Most people have little idea how these appliances work, or even what they do. To the untrained eye, they appear to be nothing more than plastic boxes that get a bit hot when you plug them in. Every new gadget seems to come with its own remote control, without which it cannot be used, but which you will inevitably lose. In many cases, the stuff is literally impossible to repair because the spare parts are not supplied or there is nothing to fix. What do you do, for example, with a broken electric toothbrush? If you're like me, you go out and buy a new one, and then another new one, and then another, until eventually you learn that electric toothbrushes are basically just a trick to make you spend more and more money.

With persistence, one may still find someone out there willing to make the necessary repairs to your broken bread-making machine, but even they will feel obliged to inform you that, given the likely price of the service, you'd probably be better off throwing away the old one and buying the latest model. To insist that something should be mended even though that will cost more than a brand-new replacement is eccentric, to say the least.

This dilemma occasionally opens up the possibility of fixing the damaged goods yourself. If something is next to worthless anyway, why not take it apart and see if you can figure out what's wrong? I have had particular luck with cheap, plastic, battery-operated children's toys, where bad manufacture is usually the cause of the fault and some strong glue or tape is usually all it needs to put it right. Small children tend to be incredibly impressed by this sort of thing, which is probably the only reason I bother. I wouldn't suggest you attempt to repair your own microwave, although I managed it once, spending several days carefully making a new door latch from a blob of plastic. It was one of the most satisfying experiences of my life – a difficult triumph to mention in casual conversation, perhaps, but I'm still trying.

While some repairs are certainly beyond the ability of the ordinary consumer, many are incredibly simple. Finding willing repairmen may be almost impossible, but tracking down spare parts has never been easier now that you can look on the Internet. You can now replace most types of remote control without leaving your computer. There are also hundreds of sites offering step-by-step instructions for making repairs. Remember: if you ruin it, you were only going to chuck it out anyway.

Vocabulary

Compound nouns: verb + preposition

1 **Choose the correct prepositions to complete the compound nouns in a–h.**

a Scientists have announced a break*through/over* in research into malaria.

b Bill Gates is a university drop*down/out* who became a billionaire by the age of 30.

c The fire was a major set*back/off*, but they still managed to finish the stadium in time for the tournament.

d Sally was very sad about the break-*apart/-up* of her parents' marriage.

e The tax inspector asked for a print*down/out* of the company's sales figures.

f Luckily, only a camera and a watch were stolen during the break-*in/-off*.

g I was expecting encouragement from my father, not a put-*down/off*.

h Although George pretended to like the present, the expression on his face was a give*away/over*.

2 **Match the compound nouns in 1 with definitions 1–8 below.**

1 illegal entry into a building (for example, by burglars)

2 the ending of a relationship

3 an important step forwards towards an agreement or goal

4 somebody who leaves education without completing their studies

5 a comment intended to make somebody feel stupid

6 a problem which makes it harder to reach your goal

7 something which reveals the truth

8 a paper copy of a computer document

Technology: verb + noun collocations

3 **Circle the verbs which go with the nouns in a–f. Use a dictionary to help you if necessary.**

a *enter/load* a password

b *insert/plug* in a disk

c *shut down/close* a computer

d *follow/visit* a website

e *click/press* on a link

f *plug in/turn on* a power cable

4 **Complete sentences a–f with verbs from 3. Use an appropriate verb form, affirmative or negative.**

a No wonder your computer isn't working. You .... the power cable yet!

b With this DVD player, the film starts playing automatically when you .... the disk.

c I didn't mean to end up at this website. I probably .... on the wrong link.

d If you .... your password correctly, you won't be able to check your emails.

e A huge amount of electricity is wasted because people in offices .... their computers at the end of the day.

f Around four million people .... the national news website every day.

Grammar

Conditionals

1 **Complete rules a–d about conditionals, using the words in the box. Some words have to be used twice. Then match the rules with examples 1–4.**

future	hypothetical	past	possible
present	true		

a We use a type 0 conditional for a situation or event that is .... and in the .... [example ....]

b We use a type 1 conditional for a situation or event that is .... and in the .... [example ....]

c We use a type 2 conditional for a situation or event that is .... and in the .... or .... [example ....]

d We use a type 3 conditional for a situation or event that is .... and in the .... [example ....]

1 My dad will pick us up if we phone and ask.
2 Buddy Holly probably would have recorded many more albums if he hadn't died so young.
3 If you burn rubber, you get thick, black smoke.
4 If I were you, I'd send an email to apologise.

2 **Use the prompts in a–e to write type 3 conditional sentences.**

Example Liam didn't revise → failed his exams
If Liam had revised, he wouldn't have failed his exams.

a Hannah got a job in Spain → met her future husband.
b Kyle's brother had flu → didn't go to the concert.
c We didn't know your address → didn't send you a postcard.
d You were late for the interview → didn't get the job.
e It rained → the tennis match was postponed.

3 **Match the first halves (a–f) of the mixed conditional sentences with endings 1–6, and complete the verb form in the second half.**

a If motorbikes weren't so expensive, …
b If Grace spoke a little Russian, …
c If I didn't like science fiction, …
d If she wasn't my sister, …
e If it wasn't Sunday today, …
f If you weren't so lazy, …

1 I .... (watch) all the *Star Wars* films five times.
2 I .... (not let) her wear my jacket last night.
3 my brother .... (buy) one years ago.
4 you .... (finish) the washing-up already.
5 we .... (get) up a lot earlier.
6 she .... (not get) lost when she visited Moscow.

4 **Decide whether sentences a–g are type 3 or mixed conditionals, then complete the gaps with the correct form of the verb in brackets.**

a We .... (not be) in this mess if you'd listened to my advice!
b If I'd had more money, I .... (buy) a better phone.
c Nobody .... (hear) us if you hadn't knocked that lamp over.
d If you'd read my email, you .... (know) why I'm angry with you now.
e I .... (still/have) that jacket if you hadn't burnt a hole in it.
f If Molly had lost the election, she .... (not become) Class President.
g I .... (go) to the cinema with you tomorrow if I hadn't already seen the film.

Listening

Part 4 Multiple choice

1 Listen to the first part of a radio documentary about flying machines. Complete the captions for the photos with these names.

- Bell
- Springtail
- Trek

The .... *EFV, made by* .... *Aerospace*

The Rocket Belt, made by .... *Aerospace.*

2 Listen to the whole documentary, and for questions 1–7, choose the best answer (A, B or C).

1 In the past, science fiction fans imagined that jetpacks
  A would become a part of everyday life.
  B would be used on the moon.
  C would only be flown by a few people.

2 The concept of the jetpack originally came from
  A a TV programme.
  B a radio show.
  C a comic.

3 What was wrong with the Rocket Belt developed by Wendell Moore?
  A It was too slow.
  B It couldn't fly far enough.
  C It was too fast.

4 The thing which causes most difficulty for a pilot of a jetpack is
  A the terrible heat.
  B keeping stable.
  C trying not to land on water.

5 How is the EFV different from a jetpack?
  A It is much bigger and has an engine.
  B It can be used for rescue operations.
  C It is already popular with fans of extreme sports.

6 What is the main advantage of the EFV over a jetpack?
  A It can fly much faster.
  B It is much less heavy.
  C It can fly much further.

7 The company that makes the EFV also makes
  A a type of helicopter.
  B an unmanned flying vehicle.
  C a moon buggy.

Use of English

Part 2 Open cloze

1 Read the text below quickly, ignoring the gaps, to find out what 'human computers' were and why they finally disappeared.

2 Read the text again and for questions 1–12, think of the word which best fits each gap. Use only one word in each gap. There is an example at the beginning (0).

3 Match your answers to 2 with a–e.

a part of a passive verb
b part of a phrasal verb
c part of a superlative construction
d part of a defining relative clause
e part of a non-defining relative clause

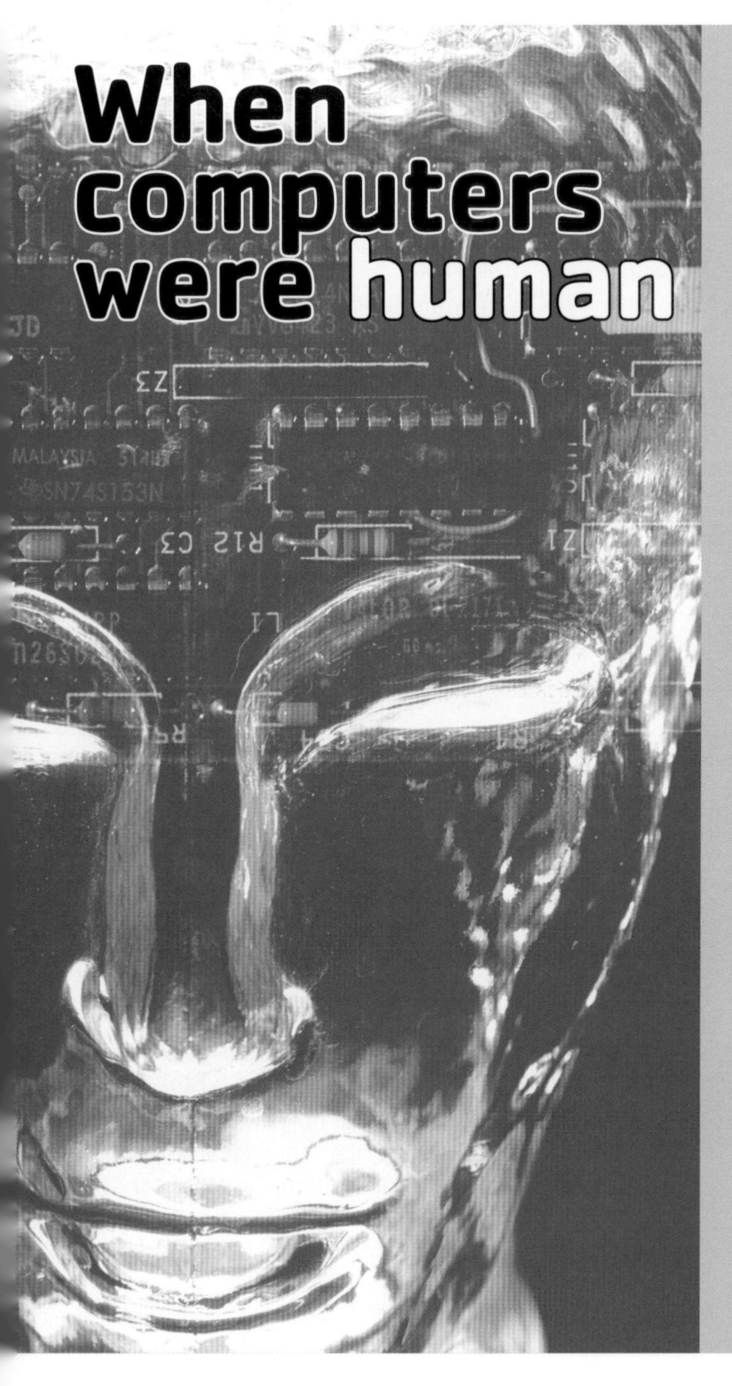

When computers were human

In the novel *Dune* ...by... [0] Frank Herbert, which is set hundreds of years .... [1] the future, it is forbidden to build computers. (This is because, in the novel's past, 'thinking machines' became so powerful .... [2] they almost took over the world.) Instead, there are *Mentats* – humans trained to perform the kinds of calculations and analysis that you .... [3] normally expect a computer to carry .... [4].

Even .... [5] Mentats are a fictional creation, human computers are a real part of history. In fact, the word 'computer' was first used .... [6] than 300 years ago and referred to a person .... [7] job was to perform mathematical calculations. In the middle of the 18th century, a French mathematician called Clairault wanted to calculate the date when Halley's Comet would return. Although he knew .... [8] to do this, the calculations themselves were extremely complex, so he shared the work with several 'computers' who helped him arrive at the correct answer.

In the 19th century, the Indian mathematician Radhanath Sikday was employed as a 'computer' by a team of British explorers, and was the first person to calculate the height of the highest mountain .... [9] the world, ... [10] was later named Mount Everest. During the two World Wars of the 20th century, huge teams of human computers .... [11] employed to work on maps, codes, and countless other military and engineering projects. It was not .... [12] about 1950 that mechanical computers began to take over, and the days of the human computer were finally numbered.

Make a difference 12

Reading

Part 3 Multiple matching

1 Read the texts below and opposite quickly to find the information to complete the chart.

	Year of birth	Name of foundation
Bill Gates	....	....
Albina du Boisrouvray	....	....
Abdul Sattar Edhi	....	....
Oprah Winfrey	....	....

MAKING THE MOST OF YOUR MONEY

A **Bill Gates**

Bill Gates is the co-founder, chairman and chief software architect of Microsoft, the most successful software company in the world. Besides being the richest man in the world, he is one of its greatest philanthropists[1], having set up a charity called the 'Bill and Melinda Gates Foundation'[2] with his wife. Born in 1955 into a wealthy middle-class family, Bill Gates attended private school, where he was particularly good at maths and at computer science, which at that time (the late 1960s) was in its infancy. He started a law degree at Harvard university and there met his future business partner, Steve Ballmer. However, Gates dropped out of university after a couple of years to set up the Microsoft company in November 1975. In the early 1980s Microsoft developed MS-DOS, which became the standard operating system in virtually all PCs. By the age of 31 Gates had became the youngest self-made billionaire in American history. Microsoft went from strength to strength but both the company and Gates have often been accused of making it too difficult for other software companies by preventing fair competition. In 2000 Gates decided to set up a foundation with the aim of improving healthcare and reducing poverty around the world. The foundation spends around $800 million a year on healthcare, almost as much as the United Nations World Health Organisation. Gates now works only part-time for Microsoft and has announced that he wants to spend most of his time working for the foundation.

[1] philanthropist = a rich person who helps poor people or people in need

[2] foundation = an organisation that provides money for a particular purpose, especially to help people

B **Albina du Boisrouvray**

Countess Albina du Boisrouvray was born in Paris in 1941 into a wealthy family. The first six years of her life were spent in New York, where she had her first experience of social injustice. 'I was in Central Park and I started playing with a group of black girls because I thought they seemed nicer than the white girls I was with. But I was dragged away by my nanny and told, "You mustn't play with those girls because they're black." That struck me as very unjust.' She attended schools in Argentina, Switzerland and Britain but left school to get married and, at the age of 20, she gave birth to a son, François-Xavier. In the 1960s she studied philosophy at the Sorbonne University and worked for a short time as a model and a journalist before setting up a cinema production company. But tragedy struck in 1986 when François-Xavier was killed in a helicopter accident in Mali. Grief-stricken, she started a charity called AFXB in his memory, in the process selling off 60% of her estate, including $31.2 million worth of jewellery and an art collection that brought in $20 million. 'The collections were never really part of my life,' she said. 'I'm not into things.'

2 Read the text again carefully and for questions 1–15, choose from the people (A–D). The people may be chosen more than once.

Which person

1 has been accused of conducting business unfairly? ....

2 contributes to the cost of running the foundation? ....

3 set up a foundation with a family member? ....

4 worked as a film producer before starting a foundation? ....

5 started a foundation with money given by other people? ....

6 has set up a 24-hour emergency medical service? ....

7 left university before completing their degree course? ....

8 had a difficult childhood? ....

9 set up a foundation following a family tragedy? ....

10 leads a very simple life? ....

11 sold a lot of personal possessions in order to start the foundation? ....

12 wants to spend more time working for charity? ....

13 was encouraged as a child not to be selfish? ....

14 got a job while still studying at college? ....

15 as a child, lived in a number of different countries? ....

The foundation's chief mission is to support children and families affected by the global AIDS pandemic. It also funds educational programmes in many countries and now employs over 400 people worldwide.

C Abdul Sattar Edhi

65 Edhi was born in 1928 in Bantva, India. His father traded in cloth and the family weren't very well off. His parents encouraged him to be considerate and helpful 70 towards others and always sent him to school with two coins, one to spend on himself and the other to spend on someone else. Following the creation of 75 India and Pakistan in 1947, the family moved to Karachi in Pakistan. In 1951 Edhi opened a small pharmacy with money he had saved up, and dispensed medicines to the sick and poor. When a major flu epidemic swept Karachi in 1957, Edhi was quick to react and distributed free 80 medicines. Grateful local residents donated generously to Edhi and, after hearing of his deeds, people from all over Pakistan sent money. He used the donations to start a charity called The Edhi Foundation. He expanded the pharmacy and opened a free maternity centre. Shortly 85 afterwards, a businessman donated a large sum to Edhi and with the money he purchased an ambulance which he drove himself. Today the Foundation has over 600 ambulances which respond to emergency calls all over the country, day and night. Abdul Sattar Edhi has earned a 90 reputation as being a very selfless and modest man. Despite the fact the Foundation has a $10 million budget, Edhi takes nothing for himself and continues to live very simply.

D Oprah Winfrey

When Oprah Winfrey was born in Mississippi, USA, in 1954, her parents were not yet out of their teens and were 95 unmarried. Oprah spent the first six years of her life living with her mother and her grandmother. They were very poor and life wasn't easy, but her grandmother taught Oprah to read and she did well at school. However, she wasn't happy at home and when she was 14 she ran away. This led 100 her mother to send her to live with her father, in Nashville Tennessee. He was strict but encouraged her to do well at school and at 17 she gained a scholarship to Tennessee State University. Her media 105 career began when she got a part-time job in local radio while still at college. When she left university she went to Chicago and got a job in 110 television as a newsreader. In 1984 she was given her own programme, which quickly became Chicago's most popular talk show and 115 was broadcast nationally from November 1986, making Oprah a millionaire – no mean achievement in a TV world dominated by white middle-aged men. As well as appearing on TV, Oprah also starred in movies, notably Stephen Spielberg's *The Color Purple*. In 1998, Winfrey set up 'Oprah's 120 Angel Network', a charity which aims to improve the lives of poor people the world over. To date, Angel Network has raised more than $50 million. Winfrey personally covers all the administrative costs associated with the charity, so every cent of the funds raised goes to good causes.

Vocabulary

make and *do*

1 **Decide whether the words and phrases below come after *make* or *do*, and write them in the correct column.**

a decision   an arrangement
an excuse   somebody a favour
a mess   research
a suggestion   progress
your best   the housework
the shopping

	MAKE	DO
1	....	....
2	....	....
3	....	....
4	....	....
5	....	....
6	....	

2 **Complete sentences a–h with an appropriate expression from 1.**

a Can you .... ? Will you give me a lift into town?

b Little Sammy has been painting at the kitchen table. I'm afraid he's .... There's paint everywhere.

c It doesn't matter if you don't pass the test. Just ....

d We can't go on discussing this problem all day. We need to .... now and stick to it.

e My brother is a scientist. He's currently .... into the causes of global warming.

f I've been learning Chinese for two years but I .... much .... It's such a difficult language!

g Chris .... He said we could all go out tonight.

h The party was really boring so I .... and left. I said I had to finish some homework.

3 **Read the dictionary extracts and decide which idioms can replace the underlined words in a and b.**

it won't 'do
(*especially BrE*) used to say that a situation is not acceptable and should be changed or improved: *This is the third time you've been late this week; it simply won't do.*

make the 'most of sth/sb/yourself to gain as much advantage, enjoyment, etc. as you can from sb/sth: *It's my first trip abroad so I'm going to make the most of it.* ◇ *She doesn't know how to make the most of herself* (= make herself appear in the best possible way).

Oxford Advanced Learner's Dictionary, 7th edition

a You can't keep missing your dentist's appointments. <u>The situation is unacceptable</u>!

b This is probably the last time we'll get to the beach this year, so <u>enjoy yourself as much as you can</u>.

4 **Replace the underlined words in a–e with other idioms with *do* and *make*. Use your dictionary to help you.**

a 'What did you say to Mike?' '<u>It doesn't concern you</u>.'

....

b Thanks for inviting me round to your place, but unfortunately I <u>can't come</u>.

....

c Sally doesn't <u>have much contact with</u> the people who live next door.

....

d She's the owner of three shops. She <u>has been really successful</u>.

....

e 'Hurry up! The concert starts in five minutes.' 'It's too late. We won't <u>arrive in time</u>.'

....

Grammar

Causative verbs: *have, make, let* and *get*

1 Complete sentences a–i using *have, make, let* or *get*, the verb in brackets in the correct form, and any other words necessary. Sometimes there are two possible answers.

a 'What happened to your car?' (steal)
I .... last week.

b 'How did you manage to carry the table upstairs?' (help)
'I .... my brother ....
.......................'

c 'Did you fix the car yourself?' (repair)
'No, I ....
at the garage.'

d 'You knocked my elbow and ....
me .... my drink!' (spill)

e 'Did the police catch the boys who vandalised the bus shelter?' (go)
'Yes, but ....
.... because they didn't have any evidence.'

f 'Why was David so late for work?' (start)
'Apparently he couldn't .... the car
.... this morning.'

g 'Your hair's getting a bit long.' (cut)
'I don't care. I'm not ....
....

h 'Why didn't you come to the disco last night?' (go out)
'My parents ....
....'

i 'I didn't enjoy learning the piano because my parents .... me
.... every day.' (practise)

Grammar Extra

2 Complete sentences b–g with 1–6, putting the verb in the correct form (past participle or *-ing* form). The first one (a) has been done as an example.

a Look at all those dirty plates! I want *the washing-up done* before I get back.

b I can't stand this wallpaper. We need
.... as soon as possible.

c I'd like .... before you have any friends round. It's in a terrible state.

d Can't you see your keys? They're right in front of you. You need ....

e John likes beef and lamb very rare, but I prefer
.... a little longer.

f Mum doesn't want .... on the line. Can you help me bring them in?

g 'Where would you like ....?'
'In the cupboard on the right, please.'

1 your bedroom/tidy
2 your eyes/test
3 meat/cook
4 the clothes/leave out
5 the room/redecorate
6 these plates/put away
7 ~~the washing up/do~~

Listening

Part 2 Sentence completion

1 **Listen to an interview with Mick Davidson, an animal rights activist, and decide whether a–c are true or false.**

a Davidson was involved in an attack on a research laboratory last night.

b Davidson is a member of an organisation called the Animal Defence Group.

c Davidson supports peaceful forms of protest but is against 'direct action'.

2 **Listen again and for questions 1–10, complete the sentences.**

1 Animal rights protesters destroyed expensive .... at a research laboratory.

2 Davidson believes that using animals in experiments is a ....

3 Firms need a lot of .... to set up experiments.

4 Davidson hasn't got any shoes that are made of ....

5 Newspapers publish .... that Mick Davidson has written.

6 Davidson damaged .... in a shop in London.

7 In one illegal action, Davidson removed video .... from a laboratory, which halted the research.

8 In the attack on a laboratory, Davidson and his ADG colleagues took thirty .... away with them.

9 Davidson doesn't support the use of .... , except against property.

10 The ADG has apologised to people that they have .... without meaning to.

Use of English

Part 1 Multiple-choice cloze

1 For questions 1–12, read the text below and decide which answer (A, B, C or D) best fits each gap. Use your dictionary to help you if necessary.

Brave nurse saves pensioner from fire

A nurse who saved a man from a (0) *burning* house while on her (1) .... to work has been awarded a medal for bravery. Sheila McDonald (2) .... clouds of black smoke (3) .... from the roof of a house in Manchester. She went to investigate and quickly (4) .... that the house was (5) .... fire.

She knocked on the front door but there was no reply. Then she walked around the house looking in all of the windows. When she (6) .... into the living-room window, she saw disabled pensioner Graham Summers asleep in an armchair. She tapped on the window but couldn't (7) .... him up. So she smashed her way (8) .... the window, (9) .... Mr Summers into his wheelchair and

pushed him to safety through the (10) .... black smoke.

At the award ceremony Mr Summers was (11) .... of praise for Ms McDonald, but she said, 'I don't really (12) .... it an act of bravery – I just did what anyone would have done.'

	A	B	C	D
0	A burnt	(B) burning	C fiery	D ignited
1	A route	B way	C passage	D path
2	A distinguished	B detected	C remarked	D noticed
3	A running	B pouring	C flowing	D trickling
4	A realised	B recognised	C identified	D knew
5	A in	B under	C on	D to
6	A gazed	B stared	C spied	D peered
7	A raise	B get	C wake	D bring
8	A into	B through	C via	D by
9	A lifted	B raised	C set	D took
10	A great	B big	C thick	D deep
11	A full	B packed	C stuffed	D filled
12	A view	B hold	C see	D consider

2 Read the dictionary entries below, then complete sentences a–g with the correct form of *lift* or *raise*.

lift /lɪft/ *verb, noun*

■ *verb*

▸ RAISE **1** **~ sb/sth (up)** to raise sb/sth or be raised to a higher position or level: [VN, usually + *adv./prep.*] *He stood there with his arms lifted above his head.* ◇ *I lifted the lid of the box and peered in.* ◇ (*figurative*) *John lifted his eyes* (= looked up) *from his book.* ◇ [V] *Her eyebrows lifted. 'Apologize? Why?'*

▸ MOVE SB/STH **2** [VN, usually + *adv./prep.*] to take hold of sb/sth and move them/it to a different position: *I lifted the baby out of the chair.* ◇ *He lifted the suitcase down from the rack.* **3** [VN] to transport people or things by air: *The survivors were lifted to safety by helicopter.*—see also AIRLIFT

▸ REMOVE LAW/RULE **4** [VN] to remove or end restrictions: *to* ***lift a ban/curfew/blockade*** ◇ *Martial law has now been lifted.*

▸ HEART/SPIRITS **5** to become or make sb more cheerful: [V] *His heart lifted at the sight of her.* ◇ [VN] *The news lifted our spirits.*

▸ OF MIST/CLOUDS **6** [V] to rise and disappear SYN DISPERSE: *The fog began to lift.* ◇ (*figurative*) *Gradually my depression started to lift.*

▸ STEAL **7** [VN] **~ sth (from sb/sth)** (*informal*) to steal sth: *He had been lifting electrical goods from the store where he worked.*—see also SHOPLIFT

▸ COPY IDEAS/WORDS **8** [VN] to use sb's ideas or words without asking permission or without saying where they come from SYN PLAGIARIZE: *She lifted most of the ideas from a book she had been reading.*

raise /reɪz/ *verb, noun*

■ *verb*

▸ MOVE UPWARDS **1** [VN] to lift or move sth to a higher level: *She raised the gun and fired.* ◇ *He raised a hand in greeting.* ◇ *She raised her eyes from her work.* OPP LOWER ⇨ note at RISE **2** [VN] to move sth/sb/yourself to a vertical position: *Somehow we managed to raise her to her feet.* ◇ *He raised himself up on one elbow.* OPP LOWER

▸ INCREASE **3** [VN] **~ sth (to sth)** to increase the amount or level of sth: *to* ***raise salaries/prices/taxes*** ◇ *They raised their offer to $500.* ◇ *How can we raise standards in schools?* ◇ *Don't tell her about the job until you know for sure—we don't want to* ***raise her hopes*** (= make her hope too much). ◇ *I've never heard him even* ***raise his voice*** (= speak louder because he was angry).

▸ COLLECT MONEY/PEOPLE **4** [VN] to bring or collect money or people together; to manage to get or form sth: *to raise a loan* ◇ *We are* ***raising money*** *for charity.* ◇ *He set about* ***raising an army.***—see also FUND-RAISER

Oxford Advanced Learner's Dictionary, 7th edition

a Can you help me .... that box down from the shelf?

b .... your hand if you know the answer.

c Our school jumble sale .... lots of money for buying new computers.

d During the storm, the crew had to be .... off the ship by helicopter.

e The clouds began to .... and the sun came out.

f Don't .... your voice to me in anger!

g Despite protests from smokers, the government refused to .... the ban on smoking.

Review Units 10–12

1 Complete the two extracts from emails with these nouns or adjectives.

enthusiasm furious frustration gratitude guilt nervous thrilled

I'd like to thank all members of the team for their hard work and (1) .... for this project. I would particularly like to express my (2) .... to Judy, who spent so many hours designing and testing our website. I remember how much (3) .... she felt when it didn't work, but I hope she is as (4) .... as I am with the fantastic result.

I'm taking my driving test tomorrow, and I'm feeling so (5) .... ! My parents have spent a lot of money on lessons, so if I fail, they'll be (6) .... And I'm not sure I could cope with the (7) .... if that happened. Fingers crossed!

2 Rewrite sentences a–f using a comparative or superlative structure that includes the word in brackets. Do not change the meaning of the sentences.

Example
You're the most careful person I know.
You're the least careless person I know. (least)

a The blue car is cheaper than the red car. (less)
b The more you pay, the better the quality. (worse)
c This is definitely the least difficult question. (easiest)
d Justin drives far faster than Linda. (more)
e I go out with friends less often than my sister. (as)
f Our exams are getting harder and harder. (more)

3 Match the beginnings of sentences a–e with endings 1–5.

a I clicked on a link ....
b I visited a website ....
c I entered a password ....
d I inserted a disk ....
e I plugged in a power cable ....

1 which wouldn't play on my CD player.
2 which took me back to eBay.
3 which I thought was attached to the computer.
4 which sells electrical goods.
5 which has seven letters.

4 Complete the compound nouns in a–f with the correct prepositions.

a My uncle was a school drop.................... who never completed his education.
b Police are investigating a break.................... at the doctor's surgery.
c Losing their best player was an enormous set.................... for the team.
d I knew the dog had been on the sofa; the hairs were a give.................... .
e At the time, antibiotics were a huge break.................... in medicine.
f They were both unhappy after the break.................... and decided to get back together.

5 For 1–6, decide whether a, b or both, correctly complete each sentence.

1 If you press this button, a light ....
   a comes on   b will come on
2 If you hadn't told me about it, I .... that CD.
   a won't buy   b wouldn't have bought
3 I wouldn't be at this school if we .... to a new area.
   a hadn't moved   b don't move
4 He would have paid for your ticket if he .... more money.
   a had   b had had
5 You wouldn't have so many problems if you .... to my advice.
   a listened   b had listened
6 If we left now, we .... at school in fifteen minutes.
   a will be   b would be

6 Complete gaps 1–7 in the notes with the correct form of *do* or *make*.

I've just popped out to **(1)** .... some shopping. If you cook dinner, please don't **(2)** .... a mess — I've got visitors coming this evening. If you have time, could you **(3)** .... me a favour and water the plants? Thanks.

I'm really sorry, but I won't be able to **(4)** .... it for dinner this evening. I need to finish some work by the end of the week, and I haven't **(5)** .... much progress yet. I'll **(6)** .... my best to finish it by Friday - perhaps we can **(7)** .... an arrangement for the weekend or early next week. Sorry again!

7 Choose the correct verb in italics to complete sentences a–f.

a I banged on Gail's door, but I couldn't *get/make* her to wake up.
b Please don't say anything to my mother, I don't want to *get/make* her worry.
c Did she *get/let* you use her car?
d The house looks terrible, but she refuses to *have/make* it decorated.
e All the children are *let/made* to do two hours of homework every evening.
f We were enjoying the holiday, until we *had/let* our passports stolen.

8 Write the words in a–d in the correct order to form sentences.

a like/immediately/signed/letters/I'd/these
b you/want/repaired/these/do/shoes/?
c Tuesday/by/need/a/made/we/decision
d coffee/I/served/without/prefer/milk

Key

Unit 1

Reading

1 c

2 1 D 2 B 3 C 4 A
5 B 6 A 7 C 8 C

Vocabulary

1
2 fancied
3 chatting up
4 got on
5 asked ... out
6 went out
7 fell out
8 had fallen in love
9 split up
10 made up
11 proposed
12 got engaged
13 broke off
14 got back together
15 got married
16 got divorced

2 *Suggested answer*
Chris met Jane one summer. He fancied her the moment he saw her and they soon fell in love. After a year Chris proposed to Jane and they got engaged. They got married recently.

Grammar

1
a are you doing
b 's going to borrow
c does ... arrive
d 's going to stay
e 'm going to play
f 'll have
g 're going to miss
h finishes, 'll be
i are you meeting

2
a have been studying
b be sitting
c be seeing
d read
e paid off
f have been working

3
1 'm taking/'m going to take
2 'll be teaching/'ll teach
3 does ... start
4 'll be living
5 'll be doing
6 'll ... be working
7 'll have been promoted
8 'll have left
9 'm going to start/'ll start
10 'll bring
11 is
12 'll need

Listening

1
a 12
b six years
c one
d none

Tapescript

Most people take for granted the ability to read a newspaper or write a letter to a friend. But a great-grandmother, at the grand age of 84, is only now discovering those pleasures for the first time, after learning to read and write. Elizabeth Schofield didn't learn a great deal at school. She just sat at the back of the class and learnt how to knit socks. She says that her teachers taught her nothing and that she was left unable to read a word or even write her own name. She left school when she was just 12 years old. Now, after six years of lessons at college, Mrs Schofield has just received an Adult Learner of the Year award, achieving 85 per cent in her final literacy examinations. But what was it like to be unable to read or write for so long?

Mrs Schofield brought up her children without even being able to read the words on a simple packet of cereal. Food shopping was a nightmare for her. She just bought things by recognising what the packets looked like. She knew that Cornflakes boxes had a yellow cockerel on the front and that was the only way she knew what she was buying. At the age of 78, she decided she had had enough and contacted an adult education centre. But what exactly made her finally decide to do something about her inability to read or write? She said that she was in a shop one day when a man came in and started chatting to the shop keeper. He had come to their village with nothing but the clothes on his back and an old pair of shoes. However, he'd got a job which paid for him to go to college and eventually he became a lawyer. Mrs Schofield thought, 'If he can do it, why can't I?' So, with the help of Oaklands College, she began to take weekly lessons to work towards her literacy certificate. It was one of the most difficult experiences of her life. She spent hours every day sitting at home practising and often felt that she would never achieve her goal. However, her friends and teachers kept motivating and encouraging her. Mrs Schofield's tutor, Alison Overington, set out a learning plan for Liz with short and long-term goals. Her long-term goal was to be able to write and reply to letters to her family who were scattered all around the world and with whom she had had no contact for a number of years. As soon as she was able to write a few words, Liz wrote her first letter to a member of her family who lived in America. They were so surprised and happy to receive the letter that they replied straight away, inviting her to visit. From that letter a trip was arranged, and for the first time in her life, Mrs Schofield travelled abroad and visited her family. According to Mrs Overington, on her return she couldn't wait to tell everybody about her trip. The truly amazing thing was that she had written a diary while in America with an account of her adventures. Since that first contact she has visited America again and other members of her family living abroad.

Being able to read and write has transformed her life. In the past couple of months, Mrs Schofield has been able to start reading her local paper — something she could never do in the past. She used to have to get someone to read it to her or she would just go without knowing what was going on in the area where she lives. Shopping has become much easier now as she can read the packets, and for the first time she can read the signs on buses so she knows which one to get on. She has even started dealing with bills and official letters. Naturally, Mrs Schofield is thrilled with her achievement. She said she never thought she'd do it and that it has totally changed her life. Instead of being frightened to talk to people in case she got something wrong, she now has the confidence to do anything. However, she realises that she still has a long way to go and is determined to do more. 'I'll get there in the end — if it's the last thing I do,' she says.

2 1 B 2 B 3 A 4 C 5 A 6 B 7 C

Use of English

1 a It includes the abbreviations *sth* and/or *sb* (meaning *something* or *somebody*).
b ↔

2 a look in
b set off
c look down on
d was set upon
e was set back
f looked on
g is set back
h are looking into

Unit 2

Reading

1 A Canada, Alaska and parts of the USA
B Southeast Asia
C Florida, California, South Africa and Australia
D Africa, Asia and India

2 1 D 2 A 3 D 4 C 5 A 6 A 7 C 8 B 9 B 10 A 11 C 12 B 13 C 14 B 15 D

Vocabulary

1 to talk about sth that has been worrying you for a long time so that you feel less anxious

2 a No b Yes c LIE[2]

3 Answers for *Oxford Advanced Learner's Dictionary (Seventh Edition)*
a pay
b nerve
c heart
d cold
e brave
f back

Grammar

1 a to study
b sitting
c to tell
d to stop
e annoying
f sending in

2 a Our car keeps breaking down.
b I really can't face spending the whole summer holiday at home.
c I expect to pass/(that) I'll pass all my exams.
d Doctors recommend eating/that we eat less fatty food and more fruit and vegetables.
e Try to avoid hurting his feelings.
f I failed to notice that the traffic lights were red.
g Sue didn't dare (to) tell him the truth.
h My father gave up smoking in 1996.

3 1 to buy
2 to find
3 to order
4 to get
5 paying
6 criticising
7 offering
8 to sound

4 a crawling
b coming
c slip, fall
d digging
e playing
f grab, disappear

Listening

1 a T b F c T

2 1 southwest
2 fourth
3 May
4 team
5 tents
6 read a map
7 rivers
8 backpack
9 high winds
10 achievement

Tapescript

I: Hello, and welcome to this week's edition of 'Outward Bound'. In this programme I shall be finding out about 'The Ten Tors Challenge', which is a special event organised by the army for young people aged between fourteen and twenty. I will be speaking to one of the competitors involved in this most demanding of outdoor races. Well, here I am standing on cold and blustery Dartmoor in the southwest of England. It is a wild and beautiful area of high moorland, popular with walkers and climbers, and famous for its 'tors'. These are large hills topped with granite, which is a very hard rock, and there are 160 of these tors. Let's find out about the 'Ten Tors Challenge' from an expert on the subject. Meet Jilly Thomson, who's 18. She has taken part in three Challenges so far, and is preparing for her fourth. Hello, Jilly. Welcome to the programme.
Jilly: Thank you.
I: So, what does the Challenge actually involve?
J: Well, it takes place every year on a weekend in May, and it is organised by the Army especially for young people. It is a two-day

trek across Dartmoor, climbing 10 of the tors.
I: Gosh, so not easy, then? How long is the trek?
J: Well, it's either 35, 45, or 55 miles, depending on your age. I'm doing the 55 mile route this year for the second time. You have to travel in teams of six people. And no, it's not easy. You sleep on Dartmoor overnight, so you have to carry everything you need with you, like food and drink, tents, spare clothes and waterproof covers.
I: So you have to be fit and strong!
J: Well, it helps! You also have to find your way across the moors. Each team has to navigate around the course that it has been given by the organisers. And you have to report to the Army check-in points on each tor. They need to know where you are, because it's very easy to get lost! And finally, you have to get back to the start by 5 p.m. on Sunday to complete the race.
I: I see. It all sounds very complicated. I assume you need to train for this event, then.
J: Of course. My school organises training weekends on Dartmoor every year, and you learn how to read a map. It's a great skill to have. And you practise hiking with a backpack, of course!
I: So what's the most difficult thing about the race?
J: For me it is getting over the rivers, without a doubt. It's my least favourite bit of the competition. You have to wade through ice cold water with all your kit and try not to get it wet. I dropped my backpack in the water once and we all had to rescue it because the water was flowing quite fast. That was a nightmare, and it was twice as heavy to carry after that! The weather can also make life really difficult. It changes so quickly on Dartmoor, that it will catch you out if you are not completely prepared for it. It can be hot, cold, windy, foggy, and snowy – all in the same day! Last year, for example, the event had to be stopped on the Saturday night, because there were high winds and torrential rain, which made the conditions too dangerous to continue. The army had to come in and evacuate us to safety. It was scary, but quite exciting at the same time.
I: It sounds just scary to me ... . So, Jilly, why do you do it?
J: I love it. It's an incredible challenge, and if you finish it, it is an amazing achievement. It really boosts your self-confidence. This is my last year doing the 'Ten Tors Challenge' and I want to make sure that it is my best year ever!
I: Jilly, we wish you the very best of luck.
J: Thank you.

Use of English

1
a at
b to
c at
d –
e to
f –
g –, –
h at

2
a At
b after
c at
d for
e On
f out of

3 a T b F c F

4
1 on
2 of
3 from
4 was
5 as
6 who
7 by
8 up
9 at
10 has
11 little
12 longer

Unit 3

Reading

1
a Mumbai, Dr Kataria
b around an hour and a quarter
c 27,000 children and their families

2 1 B 2 H 3 A 4 D 5 G 6 C 7 F

Vocabulary

1 a 3 b 6 c 5 d 1 e 4 f 2

2
a perfectly honest
b stunningly beautiful
c bitterly disappointed
d desperately close
e wildly inaccurate
f seriously injured

3
a ... doctors expect him to pull through.
b ... he pulled them apart.
c ... he pulled over.
d ... I pulled myself together.
e ... they pulled it off.

Grammar

1 1 a 2 a b 3 b 4 a b 5 b 6 b 7 b 8 a b

2
1 A: Have you ever been to China?
B: Yes, I have. *I went* there last year.
A: What *did you think* of it?
B: *I loved* the countryside but I *didn't like* the cities.

2 A: I'm sorry I'm late. Have you *been waiting* long?
B: No, I haven't. *I arrived* late too!
A: *Has the show started* yet?
B: No, not yet. In fact, only half of the audience *has arrived* so far.

3 A: *Did you see* Sammy last week?
B: Yes, on Tuesday. *He'd just arrived* back from holiday.
A: Oh, that's right. *He went* to Italy to pick grapes.
B: Yes. He told me that *he'd been speaking* Italian so much that he'd forgotten his English.

3
1 gave
2 had prepared
3 had been
4 began
5 remembered
6 had left
7 took
8 had made
9 printed
10 had helped
11 opened
12 had written

Listening

1 1 B 2 A 3 A 4 A 5 B 6 B 7 A 8 C

Tapescript

1
Joy: Happy birthday, Karen!
Karen: Thanks, Joy.

J: You don't sound too happy. Did Ben forget your birthday again?
K: No, he didn't. He forgot our wedding anniversary, but he's never forgotten my birthday.
J: So, what's the problem?
K: Well, he bought me this really expensive present- it's a diamond ring.
J: Wow! What's the problem with that? Don't you like it?
K: It's beautiful, but it must have cost a fortune. And we had an agreement. You see, we're saving up to buy a new car. So we agreed not to spend much money on presents this year.
J: I see.
K: So when it was Ben's birthday last month, I just bought him a T-shirt. And now he's bought me a thousand-pound ring! How are we ever going to afford that car we need?

2

Some of the most interesting interviews that I did were in the first few chapters – interviews with jazz musicians – especially the ones who were alive during the golden era of jazz, the 1940s. They had some amazing stories to tell about their life on the road, the characters they met, the music they were playing. I sometimes wished I'd been making a film, because the soundtrack would have been fantastic. But I think somehow the stories work better in print – and hopefully, will come alive in the mind of the reader. I've used the musicians' actual words as much as possible, but also added some research of my own, to fill in the background details.

3

Stars of the film and music worlds gathered today in a small town in north Wales for one of the most eagerly anticipated events of the year. The population doubled overnight because of all the guests, reporters from magazines and TV stations all around the world. A temporary media centre has been constructed, of the kind you normally only see at major sporting competitions. For most local people, the event completely overshadowed the local elections, which also took place today. And what is the event? After being an item for nearly five years, Yasmin Clarkson and Kirk Moon have finally decided to become husband and wife. And Yasmin insisted that they return to the town of her birth, for this special occasion.

4

Jack: Let's go to Hampers?
Tony: On the High Street?
J: Yes, that's right. Have you eaten there before?
T: Yes, I have. I had lunch there on Saturday, in fact.
J: Oh, did you like it?
T: Yes, I did. I mean, it isn't the greatest food in the world, is it?
J: No, it isn't. But it isn't bad … and at least you don't have to wait long for it. The waiters are really fast and efficient.
T: Are they? They weren't on Saturday. Maybe because it was so busy. We had to wait about 20 minutes for our main course. But when it came, I was happy – half a chicken, two baked potatoes, beans, carrots … what a feast! And I was starving hungry, because I'd been playing football that morning.
J: Yes, it's a good place to go if you're feeling really hungry. And the prices aren't too bad.
T: No, they're not. I mean, it isn't cheap but you get really good portions.

5

I first started performing when I was 16 years old. They were small places – restaurants, mainly, or clubs, rather than real music venues. The audience weren't really there for the music, and that was a strange experience for me, because even though I was quite a shy girl in every other way, as soon as I was on stage singing, I wanted everybody to pay attention. So I really didn't like the fact that everybody carried on their conversations while I was singing. I mean, of course, rationally I understood why it was happening, but I couldn't help the fact that it made me angry. I wanted to shout at them: Stop talking! Listen! I'm brilliant, why can't you understand that? I was only 16.

6

I don't get on badly with my family. I mean, we argue from time to time – all families do, don't they? I have the most disagreements with my dad, over silly things, like not locking the garage door. He gets quite annoyed with me, but not for long. We usually end up laughing about it later. That's the thing about our family – we like a good laugh. My mum and I often share a joke. My sister wants to be a comedy actress, in fact, but I don't think she's got much chance – she's got a good face for comedy, but I don't think she's great at acting.

7

WPC: Do you know why you're here?
Brian: Yes, I do.
WPC: Good. So you won't mind telling me where you were going when you were spotted last night at around 10 o'clock?
B: I was going to meet some friends outside the park.
WPC: Which park?
B: The one on Western Lane.
WPC: Ah yes, the one that suffered all that criminal damage last week.
B: I suppose you think I did that too!
WPC: I wasn't implying anything of the kind. So, why were you meeting your friends?
B: They wanted to see my new mobile phone that I'd got from town that day. And before you ask, I did pay for it. I've even got the receipt. Would you like to see it?
WPC: I'm not interested in mobiles, Brian. I'm interested in jewellery. The jewellery and other personal possessions that were stolen from 34 Western Lane.
B: It wasn't me.

8

I started working in a laboratory straight from university, when I was about 21 and I'm still at the same place ten years later. We do research into new treatments for tropical diseases. I really love it. There's a great team spirit, and I get on really well with all my colleagues. They're all intelligent, interesting people. The work itself is difficult, but that's part of the attraction – knowing that I'm using my brain! I'd hate to do a job where I felt bored or under-challenged. And for me, the most important thing about my work – the aspect which gives me the most satisfaction – is the thought that one day, I might help to discover something significant, something that really changes the world, and makes people's lives better. The research we're doing here really matters.

2 1 expensive
2 chapters
3 guests
4 portions
5 angry
6 laugh
7 possessions
8 significant

Use of English

1 a NO b NO c YES

2 1 A 2 B 3 C 4 B 5 D 6 B 7 D 8 C 9 D 10 A 11 C 12 C

Review Units 1–3

1 a up
b –, out
c in
d out, up
e –, off
f on, out
g –, –
h up, back

2 1 'll have been working
2 'm going to take/'m taking/'ll be taking
3 're going
4 does ... leave
5 'll be sitting
6 will ... have finished
7 'll leave

3 a look
b set
c look
d set
e set
f look
g look
h set

4 a paid through the nose
b he's lying through his teeth
c she's giving me the cold shoulder
d behind my back
e behind his back

5 a singing
b spending
c to write
d grab, run off
e to get
f eating

6 a after a fashion
b At first sight
c 've been out of touch/haven't been in touch
d for the best
e On balance

7 a bitterly
b desperately
c perfectly
d stunningly
e wildly
f seriously

8 a pull yourself together
b pull through
c pull off
d pull apart
e pull over

9 a have ... been learning, started
b phoned, had just gone out
c had ... been digging
d Have ... ever been, 've been
e used to write
f 've already phoned

Unit 4

Reading

1 a Central park in New York
b Christo and Jeanne-Claude
c The Gates
d 16 days

2 1 F 2 C 3 H 4 G 5 A 6 E 7 B

Vocabulary

1 a sitcom
b chat show
c sports broadcast
d quiz show
e cartoon
f soap opera
g reality TV show
h documentary

1 news bulletin
2 cookery programme
3 weather forecast

2 a series
b guest star
c host
d commentator
e contestant

Grammar

1 1 b 2 b 3 a 4 b 5 a 6 a 7 a

2 a disagree
b like
c doubt
d cost
e own
f realise

3 How are you? I hope your cold is better and you're feeling OK now. Maybe you're needing *you need* a holiday.
I really enjoy *I'm really enjoying* my first term at university. I'm now in the fifth week, and I've been making *I've made* three or four really good friends already. My room-mate, Hans, is one of them. He's coming *He comes* from Germany. We've got loads in common, and it's feeling *it feels* as though I've been knowing *I've known* him forever! The only problem with Hans is that he's liking *he likes* listening to loud music in the evening when I'm trying to read, but he's always turning *he always turns* it down when I ask him to.
I'll come *I'm coming* home just for a couple of days next month to see my aunt, who will be over from the States. I'm not sure exactly when – it's depending *it depends* on my exams – but I doubt it will be before 15th. It would be great to meet up, if you're free.

4 a *'ll be having, 'll have* two cats and a dog.
b *Have ... been feeling/Are ... feeling, felt*
c *was imagining, imagine*
d *consider, is considering*
e *will be appearing, appears*

Listening

1 1 a b
2 a c
3 a c
4 a b
5 b c
6 a c
7 a b
8 a c

2 1 B 2 C 3 A 4 C 5 B 6 B 7 C 8 C

Tapescript

1

Man: I'm not sure what we're looking at here.
Woman: It's called 'The emptiness of modern life'. It's conceptual art, according to the guidebook.
M: Yes, but … where is it?
W: I think that chair is part of it.
M: Really? Are you sure that isn't just a chair?
W: Not absolutely sure, no. Oh, just a moment. Look at the ceiling – those big sheets of material.
M: Yes, I see. They're all different shapes, aren't they?
W: A bit like clouds.
M: I suppose so. But clouds aren't green and blue.
W: It's a nice idea – but I'm getting a stiff neck looking at it!
M: Yes, so am I. I wish the sheets of material were on the floor!

2

M: Well, it depends what you mean by the 'greatest', doesn't it? How can you compare a comedy with an action film? Or a western? I mean, personally, I love *James Bond* films – I love the stunts, the special effects, the music. But would I choose *You Only Live Twice*? Probably not.
W: I see your point, but I think it's still possible to compare films of different genres. Spielberg for example has directed war films, sci-fi films, thrillers … and people are always arguing about which is his best film.
M: Maybe.
W: You need to ask yourself: how good is the acting? Is the film thought-provoking? Is it moving?
M: But are comedies supposed to be moving? Or are they just supposed to be funny?
W: I'd argue that they can be both funny and moving – and moreover, that the best comic actors, like Bill Murray and Steve Martin can make you laugh and cry.
M: I don't agree.

3

Boy: What are you watching?
Girl: It's a documentary about Siberia – but it's just finishing.
B: What's on next?
G: Nothing on this channel.
B: What about BBC1?
G: Hang on, I'll have a look at the TV listings. There's a new sitcom. First episode.
B: First episodes are never any good.
G: There's a programme about President Clinton on BBC2 …
B: What is it? A drama?
G: I think it's a documentary.
B: No, I don't fancy that.
G: That's interesting. Beyoncé is the guest star in the sitcom.
B: It may be worth watching, then. Let's give it a chance, shall we?
G: OK, that's fine by me. Pass the remote control.

4

Inventor: Well, this is it. Basically, I came up with the idea because, well, I love oranges – but I hate peeling them!
Bank Manager: I see.
I: So this is a machine that peels oranges automatically.
BM: How much would it cost in the shops?
I: About £15.
BM: I see. That's a reasonable price. But, peeling an orange isn't so difficult, is it? Why get a machine to do it?
I: It's quicker.
BM: Not when you have to get the machine out, plug it in, clean it afterwards.
I: Well, maybe, but …
BM: I'm sorry. I just don't think I can invest money in this. I just don't think it would be popular enough with the consumers.

5

Scientists in Japan have today announced a major breakthrough in the treatment of malaria. The new drug, they claim, makes the body produce a faint odour which cannot be detected by humans, but which is apparently very unappealing to mosquitoes. Although more research needs to be done, they say, the results of early tests have been very encouraging among people under the age of 18. In older people, the effects are much less noticeable. However, if it becomes widely used, it could save millions of young lives in poorer countries, where malaria is a major killer.

6

Director: OK, and … action!
Tracey: What's for dinner, love?
Mark: Don't know.
T: Aren't you going to cook? I'm not.
M: Well, somebody has to cook!
D: Cut! Look, sorry to stop everything.
T: What's the problem? Is it me? Am I moving around too much?
D: No, it's not you, Tracey. It's the lighting. We can't see your face very well.
T: Shall I turn towards the camera a bit more?
D: No, don't do that. It won't look very natural. Look, don't worry about it – just focus on the acting. I'll get the technicians to make the studio a bit brighter.
T: Shall we take a break then?
D: Yes, take ten minutes.

7

Woman: It was simply amazing. I've never seen such wonderful dancing. It was so moving!
Man: Was it modern dance?
W: Yes, it was. And the choreography was excellent. Some of the costumes were a bit strange, but I soon got used to them. What most impressed me though was the music.
M: What was it like?
W: Well, it was a mixture of different styles – jazz, classical, rock – but all put together very carefully. I knew a lot of the tunes, although I couldn't name them at the time. After the show, I bought the CD of the soundtrack. I'll play it for you now.
M: OK.

8

I: So, how do you cope with writer's block? Do you ever sit at your desk one morning and find that you just can't think of a single idea?
Writer: Yes, I get that quite regularly – although it doesn't last for long. Usually, if I can't

think of any ideas, I stop trying. That's the most important thing – not to try too hard. I like to go somewhere where there are lots of people, like a shopping centre, and just sit quietly and have a coffee and watch the world go by. I often see people who give me ideas for characters. And if there's a part of the plot that I just can't sort out, I just drink coffee and wait for an idea to come. It usually does, sooner or later. It's really important not to force it, or to panic.

Use of English

1 a the e the
b an, a f a
c a, the/– g the, a, –
d the, – h The

2 *The Mercury Shakespeare*
The War Of the Worlds
Citizen Kane

3 1 an
2 at
3 the/The
4 not
5 for
6 that
7 had
8 called/entitled/named
9 be
10 so
11 with
12 to

Unit 5

Reading

1 c

2 1 C 2 A 3 D 4 A 5 B
6 D 7 C 8 D 9 B 10 A
11 C 12 B 13 D 14 C 15 A

Vocabulary

1 **Certain to happen:**
It's **inevitable** that …
It's **bound** to …
There's no **doubt** that …

Almost certain to happen:
It's **likely** that …
The **chances** are that …
The **odds** are that …

Not at all certain to happen:
It's **unlikely** that …
I **doubt** that …
The odds are **against** …

Certain not to happen:
There's no **chance** that …
There's **no way** (that) …

2 a The odds are that Sandra and Tom will get married in the summer.
b Philip is bound to be late.
c The chances are that you'll be stopped by the police if you drive that fast.
d The odds are against this government winning the next general election./ The odds are that this government won't win the next general election.
e There's no way (that) I'm taking the blame for the accident.
f I doubt that Andrew will pass all his exams.
g It's inevitable that the climate will change a lot over the next 100 years.
h There's no doubt that we'll rely increasingly on computers in the coming years.

Grammar

1 a Mike promised that he wouldn't lose his temper so often.
b Martin offered to give Theo a lift to the station.
c Joanna asked Sam where she should park.
d William begged Jessica not to leave him.
e Richard warned Kirsty not to go out alone after dark.
f Karen advised David not to buy those shoes.

2 a My sister *told/said to* me that she was going to town.
b I asked her if she *would* buy me a newspaper.
c She asked me which newspaper *I wanted*.
d I told her *I wanted* a copy of the *Independent*.
e On her return she told me she *couldn't* find one.

3 a Sarah told Chris that she didn't want to go to the leisure centre with him the following/next day.
b Fred boasted that they hadn't lost a single match all season.
c He asked her why she hadn't phoned him the previous night/night before.
d She complained that he was always interrupting her.
e She asked him if he had ever been to Rome.
f She said (to him) that his postcard had arrived the previous day/day before.
g She asked me how often Tom went/goes to the gym.

Listening

1 c

Tapescript

Interviewer: Good evening and welcome to *Radio Matters*. I'm joined in the studio by Rachel Watson, who has just written a book about the famous radio broadcast by Orson Welles of an adaptation of *The War of the Worlds*, a novel by an Englishman with a similar name, H. G. Wells. Welcome to the programme, Rachel.
Rachel: Thank you.
I: Now, before we discuss the famous broadcast, can you tell us a bit about the original book?
R: Yes, well, *The War of the Worlds* is probably H. G. Wells' best-known novel. It was written in 1898 and it's one of the earliest science fiction stories – for its time a very novel and original piece of work.
I: And what happens in the book? If you can tell us without spoiling it for listeners who haven't read it.
R: It's the story of an attempt by an alien civilisation to invade Earth. A spaceship lands near London, bringing alien beings from Mars. These Martians start to build huge three-legged fighting machines. The civilian population is of course seized by panic and London is evacuated. The rest

of the book tells the story of the battle between humans and these terrible machines.

I: And some 40 years later, the famous film director, Orson Welles dramatised the story for radio.

R: Yes. He wasn't all that well known at the time, being just 23 years old, and it would be a few years before he would direct a major film. However, he was beginning to build a reputation as a theatre and radio director with lots of interesting and original ideas. But this broadcast brought him instant fame, nationally and internationally.

I: Why did it cause such a stir?

R: Well, it wasn't a straightforward radio play. It was done in a documentary style – with a series of 'live' news bulletins, reporting the landing of the Martian spaceship. The play started off like a music programme, with dance music, which was then interrupted by fake news reports, saying that a 'huge flaming object' had landed on a farm near New York.

I: So, not in London?

R: No, instead of setting the action in England, as in the original story, they moved it to America. I expect they felt that many of the listeners would be far more interested if the action was set in familiar surroundings. The problem was that many listeners didn't realise it was fiction. They believed the news bulletins, and thought that Martians really were invading Earth. To be fair, the radio station did in fact make it clear to the listeners that it was a dramatisation. At the beginning of the programme there was a brief explanation, and two more warnings in the course of the play. But many listeners either didn't hear them or weren't really paying attention.

I: How did the people react?

R: Those that thought that they were hearing live news reports of the invasion were frightened and confused. Many went out and asked neighbours what was happening – remember, many homes didn't have telephones at that time. And as the rumours spread it caused more confusion and panic.

I: What did people actually do?

R: As reports of more spaceships landing in the New York area were broadcast, many people fled from their homes. Others loaded their guns or hid in cellars. Some people believed that they could smell the poison gas which, according to the news reports, was one of the Martians' most potent weapons, and they got wet towels and wrapped them around their heads to protect themselves. It's been estimated that out of six million people who listened to the show, 1.7 million were completely taken in and 1.2 million were confused and frightened.

I: Wasn't it rather stupid of them to be taken in like that?

R: Not really. You have to remember that nothing like this had ever been broadcast in the United States – listeners were used to programmes being interrupted by newsflashes and took it for granted that they would be accurate and reliable. And the news bulletins in the play were very realistic, with actors playing reporters, eye witnesses, soldiers, scientists, and so on.

I: What happened in the days and weeks after the programme?

R: Newspaper reports of the programme appeared on the front page of all the big national newspapers and there was a huge public outcry. Many people accused the radio station of being dangerously irresponsible but the radio station rightly pointed out that they did in fact warn listeners. However, they had to undertake never again to use this device for dramatic purposes.

I: Thank you very much for coming in, Rachel, and telling us about this historical broadcast.

R: My pleasure.

I: Rachel's book about Orson Welles' programme is to be published next month ...

2 1 B 2 A 3 C 4 C 5 A 6 A 7 B

Use of English

1
1 anti
2 mis
3 over
4 re
5 under
6 semi

2
1 recently
2 existence
3 rethink
4 discovery
5 anticlimax
6 successful
7 natural
8 rarely
9 depth
10 behaviour

Unit 6

Reading

1 a 1 France 2 Egypt 3 Thailand 4 New Zealand 5 Canada
b underground, camper van, boat, (also possible 'plane' = l. 94 'the flight home')

2 1 A 2 D 3 C 4 B 5 C 6 A 7 D 8 C

Vocabulary

1

	bicycle	car	speedboat
boot		✓	
brakes	✓	✓	
engine		✓	✓
handlebars	✓		
ignition		✓	✓
roof		✓	
saddle	✓		
steering wheel		✓	✓
tyres	✓	✓	
windscreen		✓	✓

2
a boot
b tyres
c ignition
d brakes
e steering wheel
f handlebars

3
a went back
b pulled/was pulling away
c pass
d hit
e punctured
f swerve

Grammar

1
1 b couldn't
2 d can
3 f ought
4 a must
5 e can't
6 c should

2
a We aren't/We're not allowed to wear jeans at this school.
b Swimming is prohibited in this part of the river.
c Using a dictionary in the exam is against the rules.
d It's against the law (in the UK) for children under 13 to work (in the UK).
e The use of mobile phones in some train compartments is forbidden./is forbidden in some train compartments.

3
a Can, Could, Would
b cannot, may not
c Can, Could, May
d Would
e can, could, would
f can, could, may

Listening

1 a 4 b 2 c 6 d 3 e 8 f 1 g 7 h 5

2 1 B 2 B 3 C 4 A 5 B 6 C 7 B 8 A

Tapescript

1

Woman: Is that Wilson's holidays?
Rep: Yes, it is. How may I help you?
W: Well, I'm not very happy with the hotel.
R: Really? I'm sorry to hear that. The Palace Hotel is normally very popular with guests. The facilities are wonderful.
W: There's nothing wrong with the facilities – it's my room.
R: Oh, I see.
W: It just isn't good enough.
R: Have you spoken to the staff at the hotel? Maybe they can move you to a different room.
W: Yes, I have. And they were helpful – but they said that the only other rooms available are 'superior' rooms, and that I'd have to pay extra.
R: I see. And can you not do that?
W: Why should I? When I booked the holiday, I was told that I'd have a sea view. Now I find that only the superior rooms have sea views.
R: Well, I'll see what I can do.

2

Inspector: Tickets please! Sir? Ticket please.
Man: Sorry, I must have fallen asleep.
I: Can I see your ticket?
M: Yes, of course. Just a moment. Oh, I hope I haven't lost it. I thought it was in my jacket pocket.
I: Is that it?
M: Oh yes! Here you are.
I: Where did you board the train?
M: In London.
I: And where are you travelling to?
M: Cardiff. This is the train to Cardiff, isn't it?
I: Well, yes, but I'm afraid Cardiff was the last stop.
M: What?
I: You've gone too far!
M: Oh no! I must have been asleep when we stopped.
I: You'd better get off at the next station.
M: How silly of me!

3

A recent report on the future of transport has caused a lot of concern, especially among environmental campaigners. The image of the future which many of us have is of clean, hi-tech forms of travel – electric monorails carrying passengers silently through the skies. But the reality, according to this research, will be very different – and a lot dirtier. Far from inventing new and more environmentally friendly forms of transport, we are set to travel more and more by air – one of the most polluting forms of travel that exists. And the kind of congestion we see on the roads today is nothing compared to the state of our roads in 25 years' time, when people will typically spend up to two hours a day sitting in traffic. Despite all the efforts of governments and other organisations, the report claims that healthy options like walking and cycling will hardly grow in popularity at all. A depressing image indeed.

4

Anne: My sister's just booked an amazing holiday. Three weeks on a cruise ship travelling around the Caribbean!
Mary: Really? It sounds wonderful. Mind you, I've never really fancied going on a cruise.
A: Haven't you? I love the idea.
M: No, I'd get bored.
A: Still, three weeks is a nice long break.
M: Yes, I'd love a three-week holiday. Two weeks isn't long enough – and more than three weeks would be too much, I think.
A: I think so too.
M: I'd love to do a tour of the Far East: Malaysia, Thailand, Vietnam. I'd start in Japan. I've always wanted to visit Tokyo.
A: I've already been there. I'd rather do a round-the-world trip, starting in the States.
M: Too much flying!
A: Don't you like flying?
M: I hate it! I'd want to travel by boat or train as much as possible.

5

Of course, when I was a girl, there weren't any cars or buses in town. Well, hardly any cars. One or two rich people had them, but they didn't mix with the likes of us! So getting to school in the morning wasn't so easy. My brother had a bike. He used to cycle, but he never let me borrow his bike, even when he wasn't using it. Sometimes, I used to ask if I could ride on the handlebars, but he never said yes. So I used to walk. That was all I could do. There was a tram, but it cost a penny each way – and that was a lot of money in those days. You could buy a load of bread for a penny! Not like these days. I bought a loaf of bread the other day and it was one pound fifty! For a loaf of bread!

6

Man: Excuse me.
Stewardess: Yes?
M: I wonder if I could move to a different seat.

S: That's going to be difficult. The flight's very full, I'm afraid.
M: Oh, that's a pity.
S: Does your wife want to move as well?
M: We're not together. I'm travelling alone.
S: I'm so sorry, I thought you were a couple.
M: No.
S: Well, that makes it a bit easier. Did you want a seat by the aisle?
M: No, no, I asked for a window seat. I asked for one because I like looking out of the window.
S: So what's the problem?
M: The problem is, I haven't got a great view – the wing is in the way. I was wondering if I could move to a seat where I can see better?
S: Yes, well, I'll see what I can do.

7
With my job, you spend most of your time on the road. Obviously, you get to know a lot about other road users. I know which ones to be careful of! For example, taxi drivers are always stopping suddenly to pick up a passenger or to set one down. I know they can't help it, but it's difficult when you're driving a big lorry because you can't stop quickly. And people who drive sports cars are always overtaking when there isn't really enough room, so you have to brake to let them back in again. That's annoying. But the drivers I have most problems with are minibus drivers. I don't know why. Maybe it's because they aren't used to driving large vehicles. Whatever the reason, I'm always extra careful when I'm behind a minibus. I've seen them involved in lots of accidents. Once, I was driving on the motorway when …

8
Introducing the latest model in our 21st Century urban range – the Pathfinder Convertible. Made from space-age materials, including our strongest ever windscreen that can withstand a force of three kilos per square centimetre without cracking. Equipped with an automatic roof which opens at the touch of a button, allowing you to enjoy the sun on your face and the wind in your hair. And most amazingly of all, an engine which runs on liquid nitrogen, creating zero pollution, since nitrogen is naturally present in the air we breathe. Zero pollution. No other car on the road today can make that claim. So for a greener, leaner lifestyle – choose the Pathfinder Convertible.

Use of English

1
a even though
b as
c whether
d unless
e in case
f whereas
g after

2
a unless we get
b after her family moved
c as he walks/he's walking home
d in case you lose
e even though the weather

Review Units 4–6

1
a show 5
b programme 3
c bulletin 1
d opera 4
e forecast 2

2
a How many times have I <u>been telling</u> you not to leave the windows open?
b ✓
c <u>I'm doubting</u> that Suzie has been learning French for more than a few months.
d I'm not buying that book – it<u>'s costing</u> too much!
e ✓
f I don't understand why you <u>don't enjoy</u> this meal – it's delicious!

3
a –, –
b –, the
c a, –
d an, the
e the, a
f –, –, an, the

4
a The chances are that it will rain. 3
b There's no way that I'll pass this exam. 1
c It's unlikely that we'll get home before midnight. 2
d He's bound to phone sooner or later. 4

5 *Suggested answers*
a Please don't tell anyone.
b Put your hands on your head!
c How do you make curry?
d I'll help you with your homework.
e I think you should apply for the job./You ought to apply for the job.
f You mustn't contact the police./You'd better not contact the police.

6
a underdressed
b anti-war
c remake
d overconfident
e misplaced
f semi-detached

7
1 engine
2 ignition
3 steering wheel
4 roof
5 boot
6 windscreen
7 brakes

8
1 Would
2 Could
3 ought to
4 could
5 May
6 must

9
a As
b in case
c even though
d unless
e Since

Unit 7

Reading

1
a the modern printing press.
b a code designed to help blind people to read.
c the electric telegraph.
d the telephone (and the microphone).

2 1 A 2 B 3 C 4 B 5 D 6 C 7 C 8 D 9 A 10 A 11 B 12 C 13 D 14 B 15 B

Vocabulary

1
a I didn't want to let (*down*) my parents (*down*) by failing my exams.
b You've summed (*up*) my opinion (*up*) perfectly.
c The shopkeeper ran *after* the thief, shouting.
d I came *across* some interesting facts while researching my project.
e They called (*off*) the match (*off*) because of the weather.
f The president stood *by* his deputy throughout the crisis.

2
a come across
b stand by
c sum up
d let down
e run after
f call off

3
a turned on its owner
b to bring children up
c cut my grandmother off
d carry on this conversation
e asked for a newspaper
f didn't bring it up

4 b, c, e, g, h

5
a blink
b clapped
c shiver
d ducked
e sighed, waved

Grammar

1
1 was discovered
2 had been covered
3 had been written
4 was found
5 had been seen
6 were compared
7 (they were) deciphered
8 is displayed

2
a ... have been worn.
b ... be cooked.
c ... be stopped.
d ... have been sold.
e ... have been attacked.
f ... have been released.
g ... have been locked.

3
a Tomatoes were once thought to be poisonous.
b The Black Death is now known to have been brought to Europe by rats.
c Archimedes is believed to have been born around 287 BC.
d The dinosaurs are now thought to have been wiped out by a meteor impact.
e Witches were once believed to have the ability to change into cats.

Listening

1 1 F 2 A 3 B 4 D 5 C

Tapescript

1
Can you believe that I didn't even have an email address before I started my latest job a few months ago? I suppose I'm suspicious of technology in general – and I've never owned a computer. Now that I've got email at work, I'm just starting to get a few personal emails from friends that I've given my address to. I really don't like it when I get a message that's been copied to lots of other friends – it seems as if they're saying 'this is important information, but I can't be bothered to contact you all personally'. It's like sending a photocopied letter to lots of different friends at the same time – who would ever do that? Sure, it would be easier – but so impersonal.

2
Sending text messages can be really addictive – especially if, like me, you always want to have the last word. Now that we use text, my friends and I hardly ever send emails to each other. What's the point? They just sit there, waiting for you to access your email account. Text messages are instant, and you can receive them anywhere. They aren't too expensive either – mind you, if you send enough messages, the bill really starts to add up. I reckon I spent about £50 on my mobile last month, and only about £10 of that was on voice calls. The rest went on text messages.

3
I know it isn't fashionable these days, but I really like sending letters. Emails are great for work, or for keeping in touch with people, but they don't have the same personal feel as letters. Which would you rather receive: a love letter or a love email? If you get a letter, you know that somebody has taken the trouble to write it by hand, address the envelope, buy a stamp and then post it. You can type a quick email in a few seconds and click 'send' without any effort at all. These days, most people never write anything longer than a postcard – and you're lucky if you get one of those rather than just a text message saying 'I'm on holiday'.

4
I like to visit chat rooms whenever I'm on the Internet. It's a great way to find people who have similar tastes in music and who want to swap tracks. I tend to come across the same people quite often, and I suppose I think of them as my friends now, even though we've never actually met face to face. And in some ways, I'm more open and honest in a chat room than I am when, for example, I send an email. I reckon it's easier to really be yourself when you don't know the other person, and you don't have to worry about what they'll think of you. So whatever I'm worried about, I share it with other people in the chat room. It's reassuring.

5
I used to send a lot of text messages, but recently, I've completely switched to instant messaging. My friends and I have all got the same software on our mobiles, and it lets us swap messages with each other instantly, and not just two people at once; three or four of us can all take part in the same conversation. Whenever I have to use text messages now – if I want to get in touch with somebody who hasn't got the instant messaging software – it seems so slow! I don't know how we used to put up with it! Maybe something even faster than instant messaging will come

along soon, and then the software we've got now will seem really old-fashioned.

2 a of b up c in d on e to

Use of English

1 b

2 1 B 2 A 3 D 4 B 5 A 6 C
7 C 8 D 9 A 10 C 11 C 12 A

Unit 8

Reading

1 a encounter
b launch
c phasing out
d concedes
e consistent with
f conducted
g cynically

2 1 D 2 H 3 A 4 F 5 B 6 G 7 E

Vocabulary

1 a bread and butter
b table and chairs
c fish and chips
d knives and forks
e pots and pans
f salt and pepper

2 b and 1
c to 2
d by 5
e to 6
f and 7
g in 8
h to 4

3 a on and on
b bit by bit
c from strength to strength
d heart to heart
e side by side
f more and more
g face to face
h all in all

Grammar

1 *Suggested answers*
a 5 … very healthy.
b 1 … burning.
c 4 … cooked properly.
d 6 … read a cookery book.
e 2 … basil.
f 3 … help you.

2 a Joe can't have gone out.
b I might be able to lend you some money.
c There must have been over 100 people at the meeting.
d One of the windows must be open.
e The petrol tank can't be empty.
f Lucy might have been joking when she said that.

3 a so
b such
c so
d so
e such

4 a The weather was so bad …
b … tasted such good coffee.
c so heavy that I couldn't …
d … such a good footballer that …
e … us so long …

Listening

1 a 2 b 8 c 4 d 5/7 e 3
f 5/7 g 10 h 9 i 1 j 6

2 1 D 2 B 3 C 4 F 5 E

Tapescript

1

I stopped eating meat and fish about six months ago, having thought about it for a long time. I decided that it was only laziness that was stopping me from becoming vegetarian. I've never liked the idea of animals being made to suffer, so I thought I should stick by my principles and stop eating meat. Basically, I believe that farming methods in this country are all wrong. There's too much factory farming, where animals are kept in terrible conditions. I know there's organic meat and good farmers, too, but there aren't enough of them.

2

I've finally gone on a diet. I've been dieting for a month now and it's going really well. I've been eating really healthily, and cooking a lot more, using fresh meat, fish and vegetables. I used to eat a lot of takeaway food, and unhealthy snacks like crisps and biscuits, but I don't any more. I've lost nearly six kilos and my trousers are feeling really loose round my waist now. Time for a new pair! I'm so glad I finally made the effort to do this. I was getting really unhealthy and feeling tired all the time. I feel so much better now and have so much more energy.

3

I go about four times a week. I've been doing it for a month now and actually, it's better than I thought it would be. What's good is that I go with my friend Mick. He's good company and we help and encourage each other, which really keeps me motivated, because, let's face it, gyms are pretty boring places, aren't they? Anyway, I'm already noticing a difference – my clothes fit better and I have lots more energy. I'm glad it's working, because I didn't want to have to go on a diet. I enjoy my food too much.

4

It took me a while to get round to it, but I finally handed in my notice four months ago. I felt really good about it so I knew straight away that I'd made the right decision. Although the job was really well paid, it was just so stressful that I'm sure it was bad for my health. Especially because I worked such long hours, and I didn't have time to cook or eat properly. I was living off takeaways, which is terrible, I know. Now that I've got more time, I'm going to join a gym and eat more healthily. Anyway I've had a nice long break and I've just started helping out at the local library. The pay isn't great, but I'm really enjoying it.

5

I was absolutely fed up with living in the city, so I decided to move to the country and work from home. I'm renting a small cottage on a farm that belongs to some friends of mine, and my company allows me to work from home and do the same job online as I was doing in London. Which is just great. I love my job, but living in London was so stressful, as I had to commute and the journey was an hour and a half each way. Anyway, there's not much I miss about city life, except perhaps my favourite Chinese takeaway.

Use of English

1
a *support*
support
supportive
b attract
attraction
attractive
c enjoy
enjoyment
enjoyable
d offend
offence
offensive
e inform
information
informative
f *admire*
admiration
admirable/admiring
g respect
respect
respectful/respectable
h imagine
imagination
imaginative

2
a is admirable/fills me with admiration.
b supportive when I lost my job.
c attracted to him.
d remarks very offensive.
e more imaginative than adults.
f more respect towards your parents.
g enjoyment from listening to jazz music.

3
1 unnecessarily
2 scientists
3 refusal
4 naturally
5 development
6 unwilling
7 reluctance
8 illness
9 basically
10 possibility

Unit 9

Reading

1
a Poland
b Cuba
c USA

2 1 C 2 B 3 C 4 A 5 D 6 B 7 B 8 D

Vocabulary

1 a 2 b 4 c 1 d 3

2
a heatwave
b downpour
c gale
d blizzard

3
a strongest word: freezing
neutral word: cold
b strongest word: soaking
neutral word: wet
c strongest word: foggy
neutral word: misty
d strongest word: gale
neutral word: wind
e strongest word: downpour
neutral word: rain
f strongest word: scorching
neutral word: hot

4
a Dense
b Torrential
c blustery
d gentle
e stiflingly
f mild

Grammar

1 and 2

a *Friends*, which is my favourite sitcom, starts in five minutes./*Friends*, which starts in five minutes, is my favourite sitcom.
b The tall blond woman (who) you were talking to at the party is Gary's girlfriend.
c Can you give me back the CDs (which) you borrowed about three weeks ago?
d A local man, who we happen to know, has won the lottery.
e Ranulph Twisleton-Wykeham Fiennes, who was the first man to visit both Poles by land, has just walked round the Arctic Circle./Ranulph Twisleton-Wykeham Fiennes, who has just walked round the Arctic Circle, was the first man to visit both Poles by land.

3 and 4

a 3 I really like the hotel *where* we stayed last year. ✓
b 1 My brother, *who* you met at Christmas, has just got divorced.
c 5 The woman *whose* purse I found in the street turned out to be my neighbour. ✓
d 2 That was the moment *when* it all became clear to me. ✓ (*when* can be omitted)
e 4 My wife hated the dress *which* I bought for her birthday. ✓ (*which* can be omitted)

5
a The tall man standing next to the gate is my neighbour.
b To make the shelves I need four pieces of wood measuring 1.5 m by 20 cm.
c The youth attacked last night in the town centre is still in hospital.
d You can only eat food bought in the canteen.
e Commuting is no fun for people working in London.
f I'd like to own the house facing the entrance to the park.

6
a That's my cousin talking to Jenny.
b They live in a big house made entirely of wood.
c Let's follow the path running across the valley.
d I saw a man at the station trying to get on the train without a ticket.
e Do you recognise the man seen stealing a car?

Listening

1 a T b F c F d F e F

Tapescript

In this week's edition of *Amazing Feats* we are reporting on the extraordinary achievement of the climber, Annabelle Bond. It took a huge physical effort, and a considerable amount of money, but Annabelle Bond has just flown back to her home in London after becoming the fastest woman ever to climb the highest mountain in each of the seven continents. The feat took her to Nepal and Tanzania, Argentina, Alaska and Antarctica, Australia and Russia, with the odd avalanche in between. She scaled the summits in 360 days. Not only is this the fastest time ever for a woman but it's also the fourth fastest for a climber of either sex. According to Annabelle, the best experience of all was seeing the top of Everest.

Annabelle Bond is the daughter of Sir John Bond, the head of the bank HSBC. She was born in Singapore in 1969 and grew up in Jakarta and Hong Kong, coming to Europe at the age of eight to attend boarding school, first in England and then in Switzerland. Her grandmother, Christine, was a pioneering female climber in the 1920s. Returning to Hong Kong in 1991, Ms Bond spent the next eight years working as an estate agent. It was then that she started running mountain half-marathons and setting records, fitting her training in between her appointments with clients. Initially, she had been the kind of person who did not think that she could run for more than an hour. However, she finally decided that buying and selling houses was not what she really wanted to do and in 2000, she left the estate agent's where she'd been working and headed for Sun Valley, Idaho, to ski and climb.

A trip to Everest base camp, where she fell madly in love with the dramatic scenery, further whetted her appetite for climbing and she decided to attempt to climb the highest peak in each of the seven continents: Mount Everest in Asia, Mount Elbrus in Europe, Aconcagua in South America, Mount McKinley in North America, Kilimanjaro in Africa, Mount Kosciuszko in Australia and Vinson Massif in Antarctica. Ms Bond was twice admitted to hospital with frostbite and said she felt lucky to survive Everest after two climbers who joined their party died on the descent. In Ms Bond's view, however, the biggest problem had been keeping to the schedule, as each mountain had to be climbed in the right season. It was also a challenge to stay fit and healthy while living on little other than freeze-dried food.

She said the ascents had raised £850,000 for the Eve Foundation, a charity that was set up in memory of a friend who died of cancer. With the money she raised she was also able to pay for the education of the children of her Sherpas in Nepal. She is swift to point out that it has all been something of a team achievement, the climbs being completed with guides from a New Zealand adventure company and filmed by a cameraman. However, fellow climbers agree that getting up Everest is a feat in itself. Tom Prentice, the author and former editor of *Climber* magazine, said that it was a fantastic achievement for anyone to have climbed the seven highest summits on all the continents. He added, however, that there were many much harder peaks than some of the summits on the list. Ms Bond is aware that she has had 'mixed reviews' in the climbing world but she's been impressed by the lack of chauvinism she has encountered and said everyone had been very supportive. When she returned to London, she said she was happy to be back but was feeling a bit jetlagged. The pleasures of life back in London for Ms Bond are those of home comforts like a shower and a loo, and seeing family and friends again after nearly a year living mainly in tents. So, what next for Annabelle Bond? She's in demand as a celebrity speaker, but says that she isn't sure quite what she will be doing in the future. Although she says she certainly isn't rushing off to climb any mountains, she nevertheless wants to do something that will push her to the limit again. Watch this space.

2
1 continents
2 bank
3 grandmother
4 appointments
5 scenery
6 died
7 fit and healthy
8 guides
9 tents/a tent
10 speaker

Use of English

1
a mind 2
b mind 3
c mind 1
d eye 5
e eyes 4
f eye … eye 6
g heart 8
h heart 9
i heart 7

2
a catch the waitress' eye
b did you have in mind
c has set his heart on
d up to his eyes
e broke Sandra's heart
f never crossed my mind
g make up my mind
h goalkeeper's heart sank
i see eye to eye

Review Units 7–9

1
a My parents stood by me during the court case.
b The strike was called off when the management increased its pay offer.
c At the end of the meeting Dave summed up what they had agreed.
d Dogs love running after balls or sticks.
e Their father always picks up the children/picks the children up from school.
f Wendy felt angry and let down.

2
a click
b stamped
c gasped
d waving
e blink

3 a Carry on the good work you are doing.
b He called the waiter and asked for some bread.
c I don't know why Catherine suddenly turned on me and started yelling.
d My sister and I were brought up in a small village.
e The phone company will cut you off if you don't pay your bill.
f Joe brought up the question of pay at the meeting with his manager./Joe brought the question of pay up ...

4 a In the past it was thought that the world was flat./In the past the world was thought to be flat.
b My grandfather was given a gold watch when he retired./A gold watch was given to my grandfather when he retired.
c I was told by the teacher to hand in my homework by Friday.
d The two boys were stopped and searched by the police.
e Last year's champion was expected to win Wimbledon./It was expected that last year's champion would Wimbledon./Wimbledon was expected to be won by last year's champion.
f It is said that the house is haunted./The house is said to be haunted.

5 a heart *to* heart
b on *and* on
c More *and* more
d strength *to* strength
e All *in* all
f face *to* face
g side *by* side

6 *Suggested answers*
a such a good/great/nice
b so hot
c so fast/quickly
d such a boring/dreadful/slow
e such a nice/lovely/comfortable
f so easy/simple

7

noun	adjective
attraction	attractive
enjoyment	enjoyable
information	informative
admiration	admiring/ admirable
imagination	imaginary/ imaginative

a imagination
b informative
c enjoyment
d admirable
e attraction

8 a studying
b injured
c made
d sitting
e walking
f called

9 a cross
b caught
c make up
d see
e breaks/broke
f have
g set
h sank
i is

10 a freezing
b chilly
c soaking
d damp
e foggy
f hazy
g boiling
h warm
i gale
j breeze
k downpour
l shower

Unit 10

Reading

1 a, b, e

2 1 D 2 A 3 H 4 C 5 G 6 B 7 F

Vocabulary

1 positive: cheerful, contented, enthusiastic, grateful
negative: anxious, depressed, frustrated, nervous

2 1 A 2 C 3 B 4 A 5 C 6 A

3

adjective	abstract noun
anxious	anxiety
nervous	nervousness
cheerful	cheerfulness
contented	contentment
depressed	depression
enthusiastic	enthusiasm
frustrated	frustration
grateful	gratitude

4 1 confusion
2 fury
3 misery
4 excitement
5 guilt
6 thrill

a misery
b excitement
c guilty
d confusion
e thrilled
f furious

Grammar

1 a The older I get, *the* more I know.
b She's one of the nicest students *in* the class.
c London isn't as crowded *as* Tokyo.
d Last night's meal was more expensive *than* we had imagined.
e They say that the simplest things in life are the *most* important.
f That was probably the *least* scary horror film I've ever seen.
g The *harder* I work, the less time I have for relaxation.
h Brandon is one of the kindest and *most* generous people I've ever met.

2 a Freddie goes to the bank more often than Simon (does).
OR Simon goes to the bank less often than Freddie (does).
b Gail spends longer in the shower every day than Kevin (does).
c A Porsche 911 GT3 is less expensive than a Ferrari 599 GTB (is).
OR A Ferrari 599 GTB is more expensive than a Porsche 911 GT3 (is).
d Lucy did less well than Anna (did) in her Maths exam.
OR Anna did better than Lucy (did) in her Maths exam.

e Sandra drives further to work every day than Ben (does).
OR Ben doesn't drive as far to work every day as Sandra (does).

3 a This is the most exciting film that anybody can remember (seeing).
b Shine-X is the most effective cleaner (that) you can buy.
c This is the worst meal (that) we've ever had in a restaurant.
d In my opinion, Salma Hayek is the most beautiful actress in the world.
e Your brother is the least arrogant person (that) I've ever met.

4 1 easier
2 latest
3 the faster
4 less expensive
5 the most successful
6 the sooner

Listening

1 Speaker 1: six
Speaker 2: nine
Speaker 3: 11
Speaker 4: eight
Speaker 5: five

Tapescript

1
It hadn't been a very pleasant journey. My mum and dad, I remember, had been in a bad mood for most of the way. I think the problem was, we were going to visit some of my mother's relatives in Scotland, and my dad didn't really want to go. Anyway, we were about an hour away from Edinburgh when the car started making strange noises. My dad was driving, and at first, he said he didn't want to stop. But then the car started losing power, so he pulled over. The motorway was quite busy and the cars and lorries seemed to be passing us so quickly. I think I remember it so clearly because I was quite frightened. I was only six at the time.

2
I clearly remember feeling sad as we put the last few boxes on the lorry. But I cheered up when I was allowed to ride in the lorry rather than in my parents' car – now that was exciting. We listened to the radio all the way to the new house. The lorry driver couldn't find it at first, and we had to ask a pedestrian for directions. It seemed so quiet compared to the large city we'd come from! It was nearly dark by the time we arrived, and I remember wanting to see my room straight away. I was annoyed that it was smaller than my brother's room – he was only five, and I was four years older!

3
I was crazy about Formula 1 racing when I was younger – I knew the names of all the drivers, and what teams they belonged to. I desperately wanted to go to a race and see these famous drivers in real life, but my parents had always said it would be too noisy and dangerous for somebody my age. So, anyway, it was a few days before my eleventh birthday, and my dad said something that made me think I'd be going to a race at last. I can't remember what he said – I just know that when my birthday came, I was convinced that my present was going to be a trip to the British Grand Prix. But instead, I was given a toy Formula 1 car – and not even one of the teams I particularly liked. I felt so let down – but I tried not to give it away. I didn't want to hurt my parents' feelings.

4
I suppose this stuck in my mind because my dad has always been such a quiet, friendly person. To see him really losing his temper was so unusual – and it was such a surprise at the time, because I really liked our visitor. He was an old friend of my mother's who was visiting London for a few days. My mother had offered to put him up. Anyway, this guy – I can't remember his name – was full of interesting stories about meeting celebrities. At least, I thought they were interesting, but I was only eight years old at the time. They obviously infuriated my dad. Perhaps he thought this man was being arrogant, boasting about all the famous people he knew. So, one night at dinner, when our guest was halfway through one of his stories, my dad suddenly stood up and started shouting at him, and a huge row followed.

5
It was one of the few times I went into town with just my sister – normally, at least one of our parents was with us. I think we were trying to find a present for my dad on this occasion – that's why we ended up in a busy shopping centre just off the High Street. I remember looking in a shop window at some toys. When I turned round, my sister had disappeared. I could see hundreds of other faces, but not my sister's. My first reaction was quite calm – I just waited and looked around, assuming she would come back and find me sooner or later. But the longer I stood there, the less calm I felt! I started wandering from shop to shop, in tears. I'm amazed nobody offered to help me – it isn't normal to see a five-year-old wandering around alone. Anyway, finally, my sister found me. She bought me a bag of sweets to make up for being so irresponsible – and she told me not to say anything to mum or dad!

2 1 D 2 E 3 F 4 B 5 A

Use of English

1 *–ness* and *–tion* usually indicate a noun

2 b

3 1 a 2 b 3 a 4 b 5 b 6 a 7 b 8 a 9 b 10 b

4 1 national
2 ability
3 successful
4 Naturally
5 convinced
6 sceptical
7 performance
8 unable
9 failure
10 abruptly

Unit 11

Reading

1 b

2 1 A 2 B 3 C 4 B
5 D 6 A 7 D 8 C

Vocabulary

1
a breakthrough
b dropout
c setback
d break-up
e printout
f break-in
g put-down
h giveaway

2
1 break-in
2 break-up
3 breakthrough
4 dropout
5 put-down
6 setback
7 giveaway
8 printout

3
a enter
b insert
c shut down
d visit
e click
f plug in

4
a haven't plugged in
b insert
c clicked
d don't enter
e don't shut down
f visit

Grammar

1
a true present 3
b possible future 1
c hypothetical present future 4
d hypothetical past 2

2
a If Hannah hadn't got a job in Spain, she wouldn't have met her future husband.
b If Kyle's brother hadn't had flu, he would have gone to the concert.
c If we'd known your address, we would have sent you a postcard.
d If you hadn't been late for the interview, you'd have got the job.
e If it hadn't rained, the tennis match wouldn't have been postponed.

3
a 3 would have bought
b 6 wouldn't have got
c 1 wouldn't have watched
d 2 wouldn't have let
e 5 would have got
f 4 would have finished

4
a wouldn't be (mixed)
b would have bought (type 3)
c would have heard (type 3)
d would know (mixed)
e would still have (mixed)
f wouldn't have become (type 3)
g would go (mixed)

Listening

1 The Springtail EFV, made by Trek Aerospace
The Rocket Belt, made by Bell Aerospace

2 1 A 2 C 3 B 4 B 5 A 6 C 7 B

Tapescript

Thirty or forty years ago, fans of science fiction used to watch films about the future and dream of the kind of life we would all be living by the year 2000 – holidays to the moon, colonies in space, robots in the home. And weren't jetpacks going to be one of the most thrilling parts of our future? After eating a protein pill for breakfast, we would then strap on our personal rocket packs and fly ourselves to our hi-tech offices in no time. But we're now several years into the 21st century and so far, only 17 people have flown a jetpack. Apart from the occasional appearance as a novelty at sporting events or motor shows, it appears that jetpacks are permanently grounded.

The idea of the jetpack originated way back in the 1920s in a science fiction comic called *Buck Rogers*, which later became a popular radio show and then a TV programme. The concept became a reality when Wendell Moore, an engineer at Bell Aerospace in the USA, developed the Rocket Belt, which had its first successful flight in 1961. Perhaps 'flight' is the wrong word. Even though the Rocket Belt could accelerate faster than a Formula 1 car, it only had a maximum time in the air of 30 seconds. With such a limited range, the U.S. military lost interest and NASA, who had thought about using them on their moon missions, did not invest money in the project. Jetpacks have failed to get off the ground ever since.

However, a dedicated group of amateur engineers has continued to build, and attempt to fly, their own homemade jetpacks. The designs haven't altered much since the first Bell Rocket Belt. In fact, they're not really powered by rockets at all – they're powered by steam, which is produced by a chemical reaction. Flying a jetpack requires a certain amount of courage. The steam is forced out of the jetpack at about 750 degrees centigrade. And they're not easy to fly. Bill Suitor, one of Bell Aerospace's original test pilots and the man who flew into the opening ceremony of the 1984 Olympic Games, described the experience of flying with a rocket belt as like 'trying to stand on a beach ball in a swimming pool.'

Like most things then, the fantasy is better than the reality, but there still may be a future for jetpacks, and it may lie with more conventional jet engines. Trek Aerospace, a company based in California, has built the Springtail EFV, which is powered by a small engine. It is much larger than a jetpack, and the pilot is strapped into it, in a similar way to a hang-glider. If the design takes off, the Springtail EFV could have a wide range of different uses, from emergency rescue operations to extreme sports.

Trek Aerospace believe that they've solved the previous problems with personal flying machines. The Springtail EFV might weigh almost twice as much as a jetpack and stand nearly three metres tall, but on one tank of fuel it can cruise at about 160 kilometres per hour with a range of 300 kilometres.

Many experts believe that personal

flying machines like the Springtail EFV will arrive within the next decade, especially as they have obvious commercial potential as a substitute for helicopters. What may become a more common sight in our skies is a new generation of unmanned personal vehicles. Even Trek Aerospace believe that their unmanned air vehicle has greater potential, mainly for surveillance and military use.

But for fans of science fiction, who have waited decades for jetpacks to arrive, the wait could be nearly over. It may seem like it's just a bunch of guys playing around with flying machines at the moment, but that is exactly how the efforts to reach the moon started out. Personal flying machines, be they jetpacks or other vehicles, will definitely happen – but don't hold your breath.

Use of English

1 Human computers were people who were employed to do mathematical calculations. They disappeared when mechanical computers became widespread.

2
1	in	7	whose
2	that	8	how
3	would	9	in
4	out	10	which
5	though	11	were
6	more	12	until

3 a 11 b 4 c 9 d 7 e 10

Unit 12

Reading

1 Bill Gates: 1955, the Bill and Melinda Gates Foundation
Albina du Boisrouvray: 1941, AFXB
Abdul Sattar Edhi: 1928, the Edhi Foundation
Oprah Winfrey: 1954, Oprah's Angel Network

2 1 A 2 D 3 A 4 B 5 C
6 C 7 A 8 D 9 B 10 C
11 B 12 A 13 C 14 D 15 B

Vocabulary

1

	MAKE	DO
1	a decision	somebody a favour
2	an arrangement	research
3	an excuse	your best
4	a mess	the housework
5	a suggestion	the shopping
6	progress	

2 a do me a favour
b made a mess
c do your best
d make a decision
e doing research
f haven't made … progress
g made a suggestion
h made an excuse

3 a It won't do!
b … make the most of it.

4 *Suggested answers*
a It's got nothing to do with you.
b can't/won't be able to make it./I'm doing something else/I've made other plans.
c have much to do with
d has done really well for herself./has really made something of herself.
e make it

Grammar

1 a had/got it stolen
b got … to help me
c got/had it repaired
d made … spill
e they let them go
f get … started
g getting/having/going to get/ going to have it cut
h wouldn't let me go out
i made … practise

2 1 your bedroom tidied
2 your eyes tested
3 meat cooked
4 the clothes left out
5 the room redecorated
6 these plates put away

Listening

1 a F b T c F

Tapescript

Interviewer: Police have arrested and are questioning two members of the Animal Defence Group, the ADG. They are suspected of being involved in an attack on a medical research laboratory in Bristol last night. The laboratory was broken into and valuable equipment was destroyed. The attack is just the latest in a series of attacks on companies and science institutions which carry out experiments on animals in the pursuit of medical and scientific knowledge. But what drives people to take such extreme action to defend the rights of animals? I'm joined in the studio by Mick Davidson, who is also a member of the ADG and their spokesperson. Good morning.
Mick: Good morning.
I: How can you possibly justify the actions of your colleagues who broke into the medical research laboratory last night and caused such criminal damage?
M: Well, you say it's criminal damage, but using animals in experiments is a crime.
I: You mean destroying thousands of pounds worth of medical equipment – equipment that is used to help find cures for diseases – isn't a crime?
M: Yes, it is a crime – in the eyes of the law. But the reason we destroy property relating to the abuse of animals is to make it really expensive for the firms to use animals in experiments. It costs a huge amount of money to set up research experiments, so if we can sabotage the experiments, the firms might think again. They might think it's too expensive to set up the experiment all over again.
I: I see. So you completely support this kind of direct action?
M: Absolutely. There are many things you can do to highlight the cause of animal suffering, and direct action is one of them. However, there are also completely peaceful ways of protesting. For example, I'm a vegan. I don't eat meat, fish, or anything that comes

from animals, like milk or eggs. I don't wear leather shoes, and I don't buy anything that has been tested on animals. I also have a website and I write articles for newspapers.
I: And have you yourself been involved in any types of illegal action?
M: Yes, I walked into a clothes shop in London and sprayed red paint over fur coats. And I've been involved in an attack on a laboratory.
I: What happened at the laboratory?
M: We broke in and looked for evidence of the animal cruelty involved. We took away video recordings. The evidence we found actually put a stop to the research in that particular laboratory because it wasn't being conducted in an acceptable way. There are rules to be obeyed even for animal testing, and we found that the scientists were not following these rules.
I: I see. What else did you and your ADG colleagues do in the laboratory?
M: We freed the animals. We took them away with us – which wasn't easy because there were 30 of them – and we found good homes for them. And finally, we broke or damaged essential equipment, to stop the testing for as long as possible.
I: But this sort of violence just gives the animal rights movement a bad name, doesn't it?
M: We don't agree with violence, other than against property. Yes, we make life as difficult as possible for the scientists, but we do not aim to hurt them. Where people have been accidentally injured, we have apologised, as harming people is not our intention. There are some extreme activists out there, but we do not approve of violence against humans, any more than we approve of violence against animals.
I: I'll have to stop you there, Mr Davidson. Thank you for coming in. And now, with the time at 7.55, let's go over to the weather centre and see what the weather ...

2
1 equipment
2 crime
3 money
4 leather
5 articles
6 (fur) coats
7 recordings
8 animals
9 violence
10 injured/hurt/harmed

Use of English

1 1 B 2 D 3 B 4 A 5 C 6 D 7 C 8 B 9 A 10 C 11 A 12 D

2
a lift
b Raise
c (has) raised
d lifted
e lift
f raise
g lift

Review Units 10–12

1
1 enthusiasm
2 gratitude
3 frustration
4 thrilled
5 nervous
6 furious
7 guilt

2
a The blue car is less expensive than the red car.
b The less you pay, the worse the quality.
c This is definitely the easiest question.
d Linda drives far more slowly than Justin.
e I don't go out with friends as often as my sister.
f Our exams are getting more and more difficult.

3 a 2 b 4 c 5 d 1 e 3

4
a dropout
b break-in
c setback
d giveaway
e breakthrough
f break-up

5
1 a and b
2 b
3 a
4 a and b
5 a and b
6 b

6
1 do
2 make
3 do
4 make
5 made
6 do
7 make

7
a get
b make
c let
d have
e made
f had

8
a I'd like these letters signed immediately.
b Do you want these shoes repaired?
c We need a decision made by Tuesday.
d I prefer coffee served without milk.

What is on the Workbook MultiROM?

The MultiROM in this Workbook Resource Pack has two parts.

- You can listen to the audio material that accompanies the workbook by playing the MultiROM in an audio CD player, or in a media player on your computer.
- You can also access two practice tests online with the MultiROM. Read the next page to find out about test features. To find out how to access them, read this page.

How do I use my MultiROM?

You will find your practice tests on a website called oxfordenglishtesting.com. The website contains many different practice tests, including the ones that you have access to. Because the practice tests are on the internet you will need:

- to be connected to the internet when you use the tests
- to have an email address (so that you can register).

When you're ready to try out your practice tests for the first time follow these steps:

1 Turn on your computer.
2 Connect to the internet. (If you have a broadband connection you will probably already be online.)
3 Put the MultiROM into the CD drive of your computer.
4 A screen will appear giving you two options. Click to access your tests.

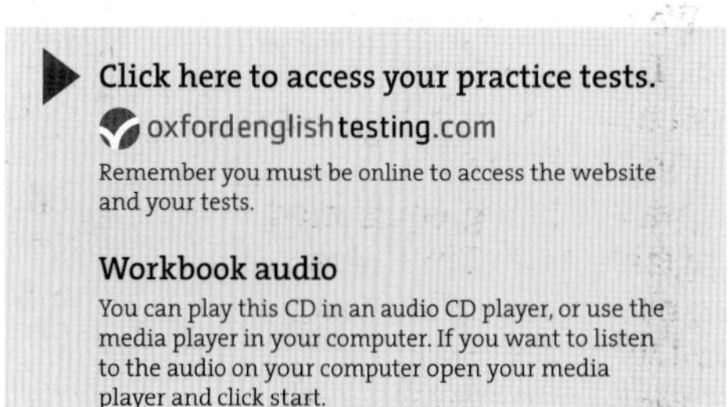

What do I do when I get to the website?

After a few moments your internet browser will open and take you directly to the website and you will see this screen. Follow steps 1–4. If the screen does not appear follow step 5.

If you have any problems or questions, click the **Support** tab. This is where you will find a list of **Frequently Asked Questions** (FAQs), a Flash demo on how to use the tests, and details of how to contact us.

1 Choose a language from the drop-down list and click **Go**. All pages, apart from the actual practice tests, will be in the language you choose.

2 Click on the **System Requirements** link to find out how your computer needs to be set up in order to do the practice tests. It is important to do this before you try to use the tests.

3 Click on the **Register now** button and fill in the details on the registration form. You will need to give an email address and make up a password. You will need your email address and password every time you log into the system.

4 After filling in the registration form click on **Register**. Your registration will be confirmed. Click on **My tests** and you will see the **My tests** page. You are now ready to start your practice test. You have three months to use the practice test before you have to submit it for final marking.

5 The website knows which practice tests you have access to because it reads a code on your MultiROM. If the above page does not appear, go to www.oxfordenglishtesting.com/unlock You will be asked to click **Register now** if you are a new user. You will then be asked to fill in a registration form and to enter an unlock code. You can find the unlock code printed on your MultiROM. It will look like this 9219e6-9471d9-cf7c79-a5143b Each code is unique.

Once you have registered, you can access your tests in future by going to oxfordenglishtesting.com and logging in. Remember you will need your email and password to log in. You must also be online to do your practice tests.

What are the features of each test?

Exam tips	You can see a tip on how to answer every question.
Dictionary look-up	You can look up the meaning of any word in the practice test. Just double click it and a definition will pop up. You need to have pop-up windows enabled.
Instant marking and feedback	When you've answered a question, you can mark it straight away to see whether you got it right. If your answer was wrong, you can get feedback to find out why it was wrong.
Change your answer or try again	You can then go back and have another go as many times as you like. Understanding why you answered a question incorrectly helps you think more clearly about a similar question next time.
Save and come back later	You don't have to complete a Paper in one go. When you log out it saves what you've done. You can come back to it at any time. You have 90 days before you have to submit the practice test for final marking. The M[illegible] tells you how many days you have left to access the test.
Mark individual answers, a part, a paper or the whole test	However much you've done of the practice test, you can mark it and see how well you're doing.
Audio scripts	These are available for all parts of the Listening test. Reading the audio script will help you understand any areas you didn't understand when you were listening to them.
Sample answers for essay questions in the Writing paper	You can see *sample answers* after you've written your own. They've been written by real students, and will give you a good idea of what's expected. The essay you write will not be marked automatically. If you would like your teacher to mark it, you can print it off to give to them or email it to them. When they've marked it, you can enter the mark on your Results page. It does not matter if you do not enter a mark for the essay. The final marks will be adjusted to take that into account.
Useful phrases for the Speaking paper	You get sample Speaking papers and *Useful language* to help you practise offline. You can print the Speaking paper from the **My Tests** page, and ask your teacher to do the Speaking paper with you. As with the Writing paper, you can enter the mark your teacher gives you. However, even if you don't, your final marks will be adjusted to take that into account.
Results page	Remember this is a practice test not the real exam. You will see your score by paper and part and as a percentage. You will only get an indication as to whether your score is equivalent to a pass or not.
Try a sample test first	You can try out a short version of a practice test before you do a real one. This lets you find out how to use a test before you start.
Buy more practice tests	To get even more practice, you can buy more tests on oxfordenglishtesting.com